Y0-EAN-320

The Biblical Case for Israel: A Christian Handbook

Main Street Books

The Biblical Case for Israel:
A Christian Handbook

© 2016 Main Street Books.

Copyrighted to Main Street Books. No part of this book may be reproduced or reprinted without consent of publisher and author.

Published by: Main Street Books

Cover Design: Linda Lanning

ISBN: 978-0-9890173-5-0

Printed in USA by The Print Steward.

Dedicated to the legacy of Ed McAteer

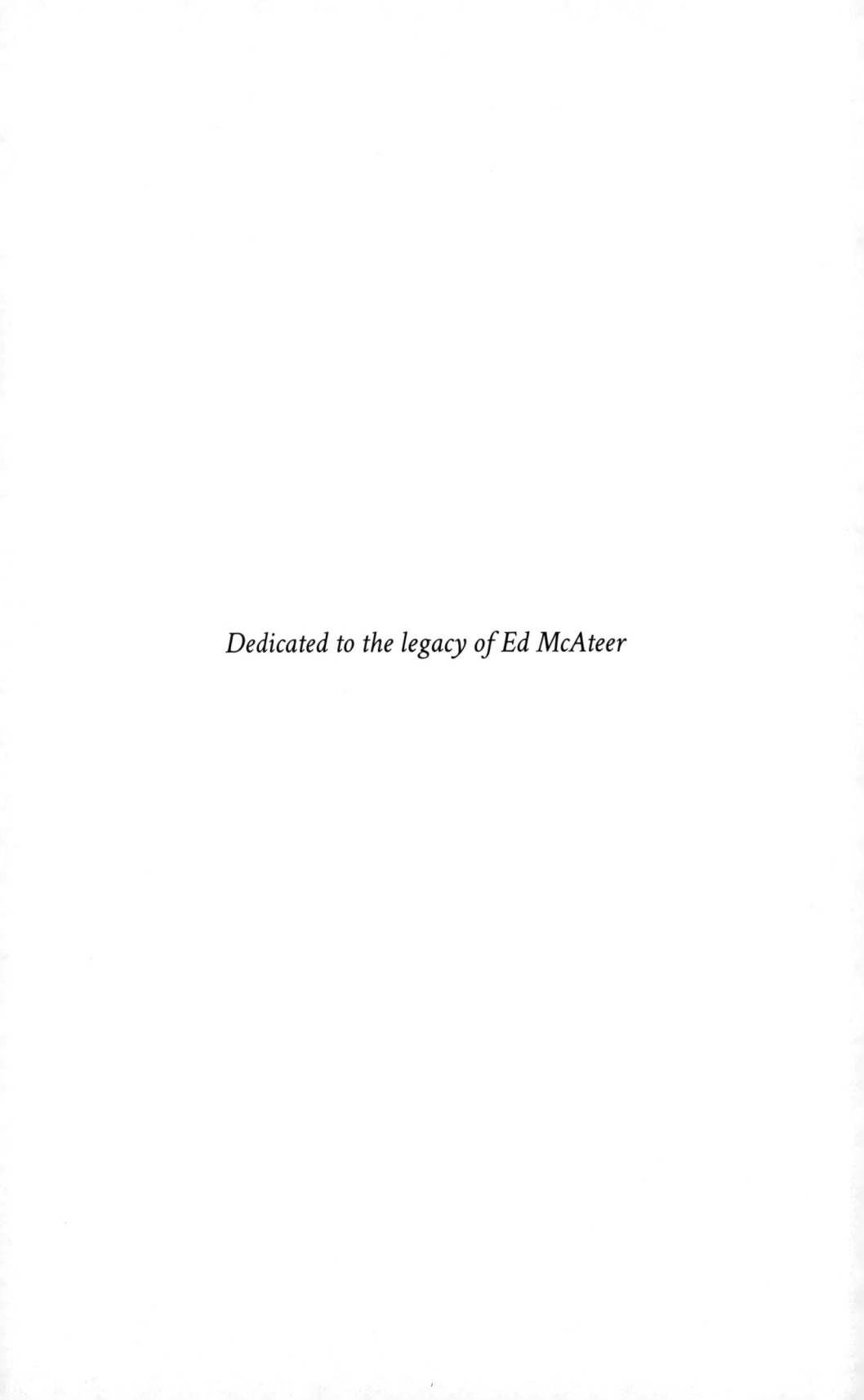

Table of Contents

PREFACE
Evangelical Christians: The Caleb's and Joshua's of Our Day
Andy Groveman

AN INTRODUCTION – CHAPTER ONE
The Alliance Between Israel and America
Israeli Ambassador Ron Dermer 13

CHAPTER TWO
The Roots of Anti-Semitism
David R. Parsons 23

CHAPTER THREE
Christians and Jews Together for Israel
JoAnn G. Magnuson 33

CHAPTER FOUR
Who's Land?
Steve Coplon 43

CHAPTER FIVE
Four Incredibly Important American Blessings to Israel
Edward Holliday 57

CHAPTER SIX
Here am I, Lord, Send Me
Earl Cox 65

CHAPTER SEVEN
The Outlandish Charge of Israel as an Apartheid State
Malcolm Hedding 73

CHAPTER EIGHT
The Threat of Militant Islam
Bruce Assaf 81

Table of Contents (continued)

CHAPTER NINE
White House Policy and the Effect on Israel from Statehood to the Present
William Koenig 89

CHAPTER TEN
Is It Anti-Arab to be Pro-Israel?
Susan Michael 103

CHAPTER ELEVEN
Praying for Israel: Why and How
Wendy D. Beckett 113

AFTERWORD
The Legacy of Ed McAteer
Daniel Johnson & Thomas Lindberg 121

Each chapter for this book was submitted individually.
Authors views may or may not be represented in other chapters.

PREFACE
Evangelical Christians: The Caleb's and Joshua's of Our Day

Andy Groveman

Readers of this book are undoubtedly familiar with the biblical narrative of the twelve scouts *(**Numbers 13**)*. The Lord commands Moses to send twelve men to scout out the Promised Land, report on its natural resources and the cities and towns therein. In accordance with the divine instructions, Moses chooses the twelve, all respected leaders of their tribes and families. When the scouts return they validate the land's natural beauty and bounty. However, a majority of the scouts, ten in number, spread lies and myths in regard to the challenges ahead – it is a land, they say, that "swallows people whole." Only Caleb and Joshua, leaders of the tribes of Judah and Ephraim, express a can-do faith based attitude and encourage the tribes of Israel to fulfill the Lord's promise and commandments.

One lesson taken from these verses of scripture is the unfortunate power of *"**group think.**"* Ten of the most powerful and talented are overcome with pessimism and a flawed narrative. It is left for two lonely dissenters to speak the truth of what they saw.

So who are the Caleb's and Joshua's of our time? The enemies of Israel and the Jews are many. They spread lies and myths and bully normally intelligent and thoughtful people into a *"group think"* mentality. Taken to its logical conclusion, their dishonest narrative could lead to tragic results for Israel – the only democracy in the Middle East and a haven for oppressed Jews from Europe, North Africa and Arab lands.

However we are all blessed that among the dwindling friends and supporters of Israel stands the community of Evangelical Christians. As the essays in this book document, Evangelical Christians are more than just a strategic political ally of Israel *(so important in its own right)*. In the words of these authors, God's word, history, theology and a heartfelt empathy and compassion are woven together in a tapestry of concern and solidarity. It is what we, in the Jewish community, call *"khizuk"*, the strengthening and uplifting of those who take on great and noble challenges. The work of Evangelical Christians in support of Israel confronts and transforms needless hatred, the cause of so much historical suffering, into purposeful love.

The work of Evangelical Christians in support of Israel confronts and transforms needless hatred, the cause of so much historical suffering, into purposeful love.

I serve as chairman of the United Israel Appeal and am an active major supporter of AIPAC, The American Israel Public Affairs Committee. In our strategic deliberations, we are certain that the friendship and active support of Evangelical Christians is instrumental in reinforcing Israel's and America's common agenda with members of the House of Representatives and the Senate and elected officials on all levels of state and local government. Many of these public servants represent constituencies with few if any Jews. Together, Jews, Christians and people of good will deliver the message that the safety and security of Israel is the centerpiece of a shared mission to promote freedom, democracy, respect for all peoples and our natural right to worship as we see fit.

In good times and times of distress, I visit Israel. It is truly wonderful and inspiring to see groups of Evangelical Christians, from many lands and speaking many languages, exploring our common spiritual heritage. I cannot exaggerate the appreciation I see in the faces and hearts of the Israeli people and in the words of their government for the outpouring of support from the Evangelical community. It is that special feeling of knowing that in both heaven and on earth *"we are not alone."*

On a personal note, I am also a Memphian, a decade's long resident of what we like to think of as the *"Jerusalem"* of Evangelical Christian America. In my interactions with my neighbors, those I meet in board rooms and those I talk to in my home or while shopping for groceries, I hear and feel the sincerity in their hearts, their concern for others and their total belief that we, Jews and Christians, are children of the same loving God and partners in the repair of a chaotic world.

Yet all could have been different. Sadly, anti-Semitism and suspicions of Israel have not been universally absent in Christian and conservative circles. One can imagine a scenario where indifference, even animosity, toward Israel and Jews might continue and take hold.

Providentially, the birth of the Religious Right was in part shepherded by a righteous man of faith, vision, good natured humor and, in the words of my father-in-law Jack Belz, *"an undying love for Israel and its people."* That man was Ed McAteer.

Ed McAteer, before it was fashionable, was the tip of the spear in bringing together Jews and Christians to dialogue on that which unites us as opposed to that which might divide us. It is all so fitting that an essay on his life and work bookends this work. May his memory be a blessing and may the partnership of Christians and Jews that he championed go from strength to strength.

Andy Groveman
Belz Enterprises
Chairman, United Israel Appeal
October 2, 2016
Rosh Hashanah 5777

An Introduction

✡

CHAPTER ONE

The Alliance Between Israel and America

Israeli Ambassador Ron Dermer

I would like to look at the alliance between Israel and America – an alliance that is without question the single most important relationship Israel has in the world.

It is the most important relationship, but certainly not the only one. Today, Israel has relations with over 160 countries. Despite the effort by some to paint Israel as facing unprecedented international isolation, it is perhaps more accurate to say that by most metrics Israel is less isolated today than at any time in its history.

The Prime Minister is wrapping up an historic five-day visit to Africa. His visit is part of the broader effort he has led over the past seven years to expand Israel's relations with countries across the world. That effort, which has gone largely unnoticed, has resulted in significant improvements in ties with powerful countries like China, India, Japan and Russia, as well as dozens of smaller countries in Africa, Asia, Latin America, and Eastern

Europe who see Israel as a great partner for developing their own countries.

Israel has also dramatically upgraded its relations with our Mediterranean neighbors — Greece and Cyprus — and after many years of negotiations, we have now completed the agreement to normalize our relations with Turkey. I should note that even as diplomatic, military, and intelligence ties with Turkey were largely severed over the last six years, trade between Israel and Turkey actually doubled over that same period. In the Middle East, our relations with Egypt and Jordan are better than ever, as are our ties with many countries in the region with which we do not have formal diplomatic relations.

The fact that you don't read or hear about that every day is not because things aren't happening. It's because Israel wants things to continue to happen.

And despite the differences of opinion that we have with some Western European countries — particularly on the Palestinian issue — we have also worked over the past few years to strengthen our relationships with these same countries by increasing intelligence sharing, expanding trade and economic ties, enhancing scientific and academic cooperation and in many other ways.

That the United States is Israel's most important ally should be obvious to everyone.

The Two-Way Street Of Israel-US Ties

Yet not withstanding all these developments, there is still only one indispensable relationship for Israel – our alliance with the United States. That the United States is Israel's most important ally should be obvious to everyone.

For decades, the United States has helped Israel shoulder our enormous defense burden with generous military assistance – something that we hope will continue under a new 10-year Memorandum of Understanding that we are working to finalize with the Obama Administration. In recent years, America has also enabled Israel to fund and develop one of the world's finest missile defense systems – which includes the Iron Dome, David's Sling and Arrow missile systems. Israel hopes to include this funding in the new Memorandum of Understanding for the first time. And crucially, as a matter of both law and policy, the United States is committed to maintaining Israel's qualitative military edge so that Israel can defend itself by itself against any threat.

Alongside strengthening Israel's security, the United States has also extended critical diplomatic and economic support to Israel — by vetoing anti-Israel resolutions in the UN Security Council, by signing America's first-ever free trade agreement with Israel over 30 years ago, and by providing essential loan guarantees to Israel during times of economic crisis.

In fact, if I were to list everything that America has done for Israel, I would be here all night. But what is often forgotten about the US-Israel alliance is that it is not a one-way street. To understand what Israel means to America, I could talk about the Israeli technology and know-how that improves American lives, the Israeli science and medicine that prolongs American lives, or the Israeli intelligence and security cooperation that saves American lives. But a better way to appreciate what Israel means to America is to simply imagine a Middle East without Israel.

Imagine if the United States did not have in this region an anchor of democracy, an island of unabashed pro-American sentiment, an ally with soldiers willing and capable of defending the interests and values that both countries share. Now imagine a Middle East with three Israels. Imagine two more countries that shared American interests and values in the unstable swathe of territory that stretches from Morocco to Pakistan. What a profound difference that would mean for America! What a profound difference that would mean for the peace and security of the region and the world!

So while there is absolutely no question that Israel benefits immensely from having such a broad and deep alliance with the most powerful country on earth, there is also no question that America also benefits a great deal from its alliance with Israel. American leaders have understood as much for many decades. Thirty-five years ago, former American Secretary of State Alexander Haig said that "Israel is the largest American aircraft carrier in the world that cannot be sunk, does not carry even one American soldier and is located in a critical region for American national security." Vice President Biden expresses a similar sentiment when he often says that if Israel didn't exist, America would have to invent it.

The Long History Of US-Israel Contention

Ladies and Gentlemen, in addition to not appreciating the strategic benefits Israel provides to America, what is also often rarely appreciated is that Israel and the United States did not always have the strategic alliance we have today.

Most people know that after David Ben Gurion declared our independence, it took President Truman all of 11 minutes to make the United States the first country to formally recognize Israel. But while some think this recognition was the beginning of the strategic alliance between our two countries, it wasn't. Truman's decision was an historic act of moral clarity. But it came at a time when an American arms embargo was being imposed on a fledgling Jewish state fighting for its life against five invading Arab armies.

Remember, in 1948, Israel fought its War of Independence with Czech rifles. Two decades later, Israel flew French fighter planes during the Six Day War.

The truth is that the strategic alliance between our two countries began to be forged only after Israel proved its prowess and resiliency on the battlefield. Only then did American policymakers begin to appreciate that Israel was not merely a moral cause but also a strategic asset. What had started out as a moral imperative of some to help the Jewish people overcome the horrors of the past soon turned into an effort by many to strengthen a reliable ally that could help America address both present and future challenges in the Middle East. That was true for the last two decades of the Cold War and that has been true since the rise of militant Islam as a force in the region and the world, particularly since 9/11.

Now, some of you may be saying to yourselves that that is all well and good but that this sentiment is a product of the past. Today, some will argue, Israel and the United States have serious disagreements on important issues that will ultimately fray our strategic alliance. History suggests otherwise. The truth is that the alliance between America and Israel grew from a moral commitment to a strategic partnership despite having to weather many serious disagreements along the way, even on vital issues.

In 1948, then Secretary of State George Marshall warned the soon-to-be Israeli government not to declare its independence.

In 1967, as Nasser was tightening the noose around IsIrael's neck, President Johnson made clear to Israel that if it acted alone, it would be alone.

In 1981, after Israel bombed the Osirak nuclear reactor, the Reagan administration joined in condemning Israel at the UN Security Council and held up arms transfers to Israel for three months.

In 2002, after Israel responded to the worst terror campaign in its history, by launching Operation Defensive Shield, the Bush administration insisted that Israel withdraw its forces immediately from all Palestinian areas.

These are only a few of the many instances when there was serious turbulence in the US-Israel relationship. But despite these bumps, the alliance between America and Israel grew stronger and our friendship grew deeper, decade after decade. And I believe our alliance will continue to grow stronger and deeper in the years ahead despite the serious disagreement Israel has with the Obama Administration over the best way to prevent a nuclear armed Iran.

Diverging on Iran

I don't want to spend too much time rehashing the debate over the nuclear deal with Iran. But the differences remain clear. The Obama Administration sincerely believes the nuclear deal with Iran makes America and Israel safer. Israel disagrees. The Obama Administration believes that this deal blocks Iran's path to the bomb. Israel believes that the deal ultimately paves Iran's path to the bomb.

The best that can honestly be said about this deal is that it may temporarily block that path. Yet the price for that temporary delay is not only removing the tough sanctions that were crippling the economy of the world's leading sponsor of terrorism. The even heavier price is that in 10 to 15 years, Iran will have a fully legitimate industrial-sized nuclear enrichment program, as the restrictions placed on Iran's nuclear program are automatically removed. Those two words – *"automatically removed"* – are at the heart of Israel's opposition to the deal.

All the restrictions the deal puts in place will be automatically removed even if Iran's regime continues its aggression against its neighbors, continues its support for terror across the world and continues its commitment in both word and deed to annihilate Israel. No amount of spin can change the fact that in 15 years, Iran will be able to spin as much uranium as it wants without consequence. And as the Prime Minister said last year in his speech to Congress, 15 years may seem like a long time in politics, but it is a blink of an eye in the life of a nation.

Partners In Security And Tech Innovation

Still, despite the profound disagreement between Israel and the Obama Administration on such a vital issue — as well as ongoing disagreements on the best way to advance peace with the Palestinians — I am confident that the alliance between America and Israel will continue to grow stronger in the years ahead. First, because the most dangerous security challenges facing the United States will continue to emanate from the Middle East for a long time to come. Some in the United States hope that America can pivot away from the Middle East. But for the foreseeable future, I don't think the Middle East is going to pivot away from America. In the coming years, Israel's importance to America as a reliable ally and a formidable military power in a very dangerous region is likely to become more critical not less critical for protecting America's security interests. In fact, the fewer troops America has on the ground in the Middle East, the more important having a reliable Israeli ally becomes.

Second, the 21st century is a century of knowledge, in which prosperity in the developed world will be driven primarily by a country's ability to innovate. There are two great centers of innovation in the world today. One is in Silicon Valley. The second is here in Israel. In the coming years and decades, Israel's value as a leader in technology — in medicine, science, agriculture, water and cyber — will continue to cement our relations with countries around the world, including America.

The statistic that I think most powerfully illustrates Israel's disproportionate value as an ally in technology is what is happening in cyber. In 2014, Israel accounted for over 10% of global investments in cybersecurity. Think about that. Israel is 1/10th of 1% of the world's population. But in cyber, Israel in 2014 was punching 100 times above its weight. That sounds impressive. But in 2015, that number jumped to 20%. That means

Israel is punching 200 times above its weight. So in cyber, do not think of Israel as a small country of 8.5 million people. In cyber, Israel is a China.

And as the United States looks at the top cyber powers, the only one that is a potential ally is Israel.

While most people seem to appreciate the hasbara value of Israel being branded the start-up nation, fewer seem to fully appreciate the strategic significance of the technology ecosystem that has been created in Israel. America's leading technology companies — the Intels, Microsofts, Apples, Googles and dozens of others — are not in Israel because they are Zionists. They are here because they want to tap into our remarkable culture of innovation and position themselves to continue to lead the world into the next century. That is why the BDS movement will ultimately fail, and that is also one of the reasons why Israel's alliance with America will continue to grow stronger.

In fact, I believe that for these two reasons alone – security and technology – Israel is likely to be America's most important ally in the 21st century. I know that's a strong statement. But if an Israeli Ambassador would have stood here thirty years ago and said that Israel would become a global technological power, it would have sounded no less farfetched. But that happened. And if that same Ambassador would have also told you that Israel would one day be selling gas to its neighbors that would have sounded downright crazy. But that's going to happen as well.

In fact, the significant energy resources we have discovered — and may yet discover — will not only enhance Israel's strategic position in the region, it will affect our relationship with the United States as well by turning Israel into an even more powerful ally.

An Alliance Of Shared Values

Beyond security and technology, my confidence in the future of the US-Israel alliance also comes from my appreciation that our alliance is rooted in things that run much deeper. It is rooted in our most cherished values and in a shared sense of destiny. The idea that all are created equal in the image of God, that no one is above the law, that compassion for the most vulnerable is a sacred obligation — ideas which have been a moral compass for generations of Americans — were ideas first championed thousands of years ago by the prophets of the Jewish people and which today are fused into the national identity of the Jewish state.

As so much of the Middle East continues its descent into chaos and barbarism, as our values come under further attack in a region where women are treated like chattel, Christians are beheaded en masse, minority populations are decimated, and gays are hanged in town squares, Israel will increasingly stand out as a beacon of humanity and decency. This will inevitably bring America and Israel closer together.

But there is something even beyond interests and values that goes to the very core of the unique alliance between Israel and America. You see, both America and Israel are not merely countries. They are also causes. America has long been what Lincoln called the last best hope on earth — a beacon of opportunity for people across the world, carrying the torch of freedom for all humanity and entrusted by history with securing liberty's future.

Israel is the hope of the Jewish people, offering opportunity for all its citizens — Jewish and non-Jewish alike — safeguarding freedom in the darkest region on earth and entrusted by history with securing the Jewish future.

These causes imbue each country with a deep sense of purpose – and because these purposes are not at odds with each other but rather complement and reinforce one another, they also imbue the two countries with a deep sense of solidarity. That is why I believe tens of millions of Americans support Israel in a way they support no other country in the world and why Israelis mourn America's tragedies and rejoice in America's triumphs as perhaps no other country in the world does. That is why from New York to California, from Alabama to Montana, Israel resonates with Americans in a way no other country does and why so many Israelis fly American flags on our own Independence Day.

I believe that to truly appreciate the unique alliance between America and Israel, you must appreciate what having such a sense of purpose means to both countries. Those who don't share this sense of purpose or who are too cynical to even believe in a sense of purpose will never truly appreciate the power of the friendship between America and Israel. But this sense of purpose is bigger than any leader or any issue. It is the

DNA of both countries and it lies at the bedrock of our unique alliance.

That is why the real danger to this alliance will not come from disagreements over policy, demographic changes, or the numerous other reasons that are routinely cited as potential signs of trouble. The real danger would be for either America or Israel to lose its sense of purpose, for either country to no longer believe in its own exceptionalism. It would come if those who work day in and day out to tear down that sense of exceptionalism succeed.

I believe they won't succeed. I believe that the sense of purpose of both countries will continue to remain strong. In fact, it may even get stronger in the face of a fanaticism that is lashing out across the world, from San Bernadino and Orlando to Paris and Brussels to Istanbul, Tel Aviv and Hebron. And with that strong sense of purpose buttressed by common interests and anchored in shared values, I believe that the alliance between Israel and America will become stronger than ever.

Ron Dermer is Israel's Ambassador to the United States. The above remarks were delivered on July 7, 2016, at the B'nai B'rith World Center Award for Journalism ceremony in Jerusalem and have been reprinted with permission.

CHAPTER TWO

The Roots of Anti-Semitism

David R. Parsons

It seems odd that a chapter of this nature would even be necessary. Why should we have to defend the very right to exist of a modern, free democratic nation with a well-known history going back thousands of years? What other nation on earth today is incessantly badgered, demonized and defamed as is Israel? Indeed, her basic legitimacy is called into question on a daily basis all around the globe by some very determined adversaries. Thus the need for people of goodwill to come to her defense. And in standing up for the Jewish state on biblical, moral and historical grounds, the contributors to this book are confronting an ancient, vile prejudice known as anti-Semitism. If there were no anti-Semites in the world, then pro-Israel works such as this collection of essays would not be so necessary. But alas, we have no choice other than to engage her enemies and dispel their lies and distortions. And one notable and effective way of doing so is to expose Israel's detractors as merely carrying on a very dark and bitter legacy. Anti-Semitism has rightly been labeled "mankind's oldest hatred," and it has left a long, sordid trail of death and destruction in its wake. Yet this hatred is as resurgent as ever today, taking aim not only at individual Jews around the world but also lashing out against the "collective Jew" represented by the nation of Israel.

In recent decades there has been an upsurge in violence and incitement against Jews all over the world, especially in Europe. Jewish communities across the continent have been advised not to wear kippas or other religious symbols in public anymore. Every Jewish synagogue and community center has had to post armed guards at their entrances. Some claim Europe is becoming as dangerous for Jews as Germany in the 1930s. And the threat extends even to such far off places as Australia, where a group of Jews in the quaint beach resort town of Bondi were recently assaulted and severely beaten while coming out of a synagogue on Shabbat.

Meanwhile, the campaign to delegitimize the state of Israel is relentless. The legal, diplomatic and economic warfare against the Jewish state is intensifying. Even the United Nations itself has become a major purveyor of anti-Semitism, as its various organs are openly manipulated to unfairly issue repeated condemnations of Israel, a liberal democracy, while repressive and tyrannical regimes elsewhere go unscathed.

Such manifestations of anti-Semitism are nothing new. This malady has a long and tragic past which goes back thousands of years. From one generation to the next, history is replete with examples of people who have harbored an inexplicable hatred towards the Jews and who have sought to justify this hostility in contrived ways. Thus scholars have studied the phenomenon in hopes of understanding its root causes, with some approaching it as something of a mental disorder which could perhaps be cured with the right treatments. Experts have identified several distinct types of this ancient hatred which have emerged over time – namely religious, racial and conspiratorial anti-Semitism. There was some hope that the grave atrocities of the Holocaust might lead to a decline in anti-Semitism, yet all three forms are still prevalent in the post-Holocaust era. Even worse, it often surfaces today as an odious mixture of all three types – religious bigotry blended with racial animus and outlandish conspiracy theories.

Still, trying to understand and treat the root causes of anti-Semitism is not an exact science. This is because it is largely grounded in an irrational hatred, given that there is no sane reason for all the slandering and scapegoating of the Jewish people. During my time as a pro-Israel lobbyist in Washington, DC in the early 1990s, I can recall hearing UN Ambassador Jeane Kirkpatrick speak of her time as the top US representative at the United Nations. She spoke of encountering a visceral hatred of Israel there among educated, cultured diplomats at the United Nations which was utterly *"mysterious."* There was simply no rationale for it, yet she said it pervaded the entire institution. This should come as no surprise, however, since what we are dealing with is really a spiritual malady. At its root, anti-Semitism is a spirit of jealousy and rejection operating against the Jewish people and every person in every generation has the choice of whether to agree with that spirit or not. Sadly, too many have listened to this lying voice and turned on the Jews. As we look back through this tragic history, the sheer absurdity of anti-Semitic beliefs and accusations becomes apparent.

Religious Anti-Semitism

Hatred of the Jewish people based on religious grounds is usually attributed first and foremost to Christians. There is much truth to this charge, as the horrific atrocities committed against Jews in the name of Christ are probably the greatest stain on the Church in its 2,000 year-old history. From the time of the Council of Nicea in 325 AD, the Gentile-dominated Church deliberately severed itself from its Hebraic roots and rejected the Jews as Christ-killers. This gave rise to Replacement theology or Supersessionism, and the *"teaching of contempt"* against the Jews. The Roman exile and dispersion of the Jews was taken as an enduring sign of their permanent rejection by God for having committed Deicide, with the Church superseding or replacing Israel as God's sole redemptive agent in the world. The malevolent fruit of this hostile attitude among Christians included pogroms, forced conversions, massacres, inquisitions and expulsions, right up to the Holocaust.

Yet Jesus himself was Jewish, as were nearly all the early believers in Christ and the writers of the New Testament. The Apostle Paul also had specifically forewarned Gentile believers not to be arrogant towards the Jews, but rather to be humble and grateful, and to show them mercy *(Romans 11:12-32; 15:27).* In addition, we need to realize that the early Gentile fathers of the Church grossly misread redemptive history. They either forgot or ignored the Apostles' teachings that the Jewish rejection of Jesus was foreordained by God for a greater purpose, as was their rejection of the Gospel (Acts 3:17-21; Romans 11:28-29). How else would Jesus have made it to the cross for our sake, and how else would the Gospel have gone out to all nations? Further, every single day of Israel's exile and dispersion God was being faithful to His side of the deal agreed to at Sinai. The covenant mediated through Moses held that if the people of Israel were faithful and obedient, then God would deliver the Promised Land to them in rest and peace. But if they were unfaithful and disobedient, He would exile them from the land and they would not find a place among the nations in which to rest their feet. So every day of their exile, God was just being faithful to His end of the bargain and He never once broke covenant with the Jewish people. Yet God also promised that no matter how far He scattered them, He would one day come find the Jews and bring them back to the land He promised to their forefathers (Leviticus 26:40-45; Deuteronomy 30:1-10; Jeremiah 31:10; Ezekiel 20:33-44; 36:16-33).

So we see there was no biblical reason or justification for all those centuries of Christian anti-Semitism. Yet it poisoned successive generations of Christians and even prominent leaders of the Church, such as the reformer Martin Luther. When Luther was immersed in his great work of translating the Bible from the original Hebrew and Greek into the common German tongue, he consulted regularly with local Jewish rabbis and gradually developed a relationship with them. But later, when he tried to convince them to accept his revelation of the just living by faith in Christ, they rejected it and he in turn rejected them. Thus in the latter part of his career, Luther turned against the Jews and even authored a spiteful anti-Semitic treatise entitled On the Jews and Their Lies. In this shameful screed, he called for the burning of Jewish homes, schools and synagogues, for destroying their prayer books, seizing their money and property, and forbidding rabbis to preach. Luther also cited the scattering and dispersion of the Jews as standing proof that they were indeed cursed by God forever. But what would Luther say today, with roughly half the Jews in the world now regathered back in the land and living under restored Jewish sovereignty? Again, this is a case of Christians misreading redemptive history, and God proving Himself ever faithful to His covenant with Israel.

Now the Christian world does not have a monopoly on religious anti-Semitism, as Islam has its own uniquely vile history of hatred and bigotry towards the Jewish people. Both the Koran and the hadiths (early traditions associated with Muhammed) contain overtly anti-Semitic passages and teachings. The Jews are presented as inherently evil and untrustworthy for having deceived the prophet. They are degraded as inhuman, the descendants of monkeys and pigs. They are accused of falsifying portions of the Old Testament. And they are seen as predestined to be in constant warfare with the followers of Islam until a tribe of Muslims finally rises up and wipes them out completely in order to bring on Judgment Day.

Much of this Islamic anti-Semitism can be traced back to the prophet Muhammed going through a similar experience as Martin Luther with his Jewish acquaintances. Scholars say Muhammed had Jewish tutors growing up and also befriended a tribe of Jews as he prepared his army in Medina for the assault on the idol worship center in Mecca. But when this local Jewish tribe would not accept his revelations from Allah and join his military campaign, he turned on them and wiped them out. Thus during the latter half of his career, Muhammed was very anti-Semitic in his attitude and Koranic pronouncements. This all has led to centuries of Islamic persecution and oppression of Jews throughout the Middle East and North Africa. It was officially enshrined in shari'a law and in the dhimmi system set up in the Islamic crescent. Yet, once again, there was no rational basis for any of these false claims and hostile views towards the Jewish people. Multitudes were deceived once more into suspending reality and agreeing with a spirit of rejection against the children of Israel.

Racial Anti-Semitism

In more modern times, we have seen the rise of an odious loathing of the Jewish people based on racial grounds, most notably in Nazi Germany. Aryanism, the theory that the Aryan or Nordic peoples of northern European are inherently superior to all other races gained great popularity in Germany even before Adolf Hitler rose to power. This radical belief in a German Master Race owed its wider acceptance to the advent of Darwinian evolution, as biologists such as Ernst Haeckel and historians such as Houston Stewart Chamberlain adapted Charles Darwin's views to bolster their claims to Aryan supremacy. In this way, racial hatred against Jews, blacks and other "inferior" races was given a scientific veneer, making them more palatable to the German masses.

Now it is true that many Christians across Europe became willing accomplices with Hitler and the Nazis in their genocidal campaign against European Jewry. This was because after centuries of Christian anti-Semitic teachings they had become accustomed to despising the Jews. Yet the Nazi movement itself was essentially pagan, having rejected Christianity as too moral and weak for the worldwide German empire they sought to build. Instead, the Nazis blended a mystical belief in Aryan supremacy with Darwinian evolutionary thinking in order to justify their plans to exterminate the Jews of Europe. In fact, Hitler's manifesto Mein Kampf does not contain one scripture quote, but rather it reads like a biological paper. Even the title, meaning "My Struggle," refers to the biological struggle of the German race for the resources needed to survive the battle of natural selection over other races and to prevent regression of their species due to mixing with inferior peoples, especially the Jews.

Here again, we see one of the main trademarks of anti-Semitism: it is an irrational hatred and rejection of the Jewish people which likes to hide behind a façade, whether it be religion, science or some other false validation for detesting the Jews.

Conspiratorial Anti-Semitism

The Nazis also merged their racial animus toward the Jewish people with a new brand of conspiratorial anti-Semitism which promoted a false narrative that the Jews were plotting to control the world. This vicious libel actually originated in czarist Russia in the late 1800s and was encapsulated in the booklet entitled The Protocols of the Learned Elders of Zion. Forged by an agent of the czar's secret police, the pamphlet purported to be the minutes of a secret meeting at the First Zionist Congress in 1897, at which a cabal of Jewish leaders plotted to take over the world. They were said to have conspired to use Communism, materialism, world wars, economic depressions, pornography and other means to achieve global control.

Although later proven to be a total forgery, The Protocols were still circulating in Germany during the post-World War I period when the nation was beset by hyper-inflation and highly resentful of the heavy price it was forced to pay for losing that conflict. A young Adolf Hitler seized on this Zionist conspiracy theory and falsely blamed the Jews for Germany's humiliation and defeat. Within a decade, he held dictatorial powers over Germany and began plotting the conquest of Europe and the extermination of its Jewish populations. Much of the Nazi propaganda was aimed at preparing the people for this coming bloodbath by presenting the Jews as racially inferior, and yet diabolically clever enough to pursue world dominance. They mastered the merging of racial and conspiratorial anti-Semitism in a way that paved the path for the Holocaust.

> **Anti-Semitism has not disappeared in the post-Holocaust era. Instead it has re-emerged as strong as ever in the form of anti-Zionism or anti-Israelism**

Anti-Semitism In The Post-Holocaust Era

Once the depravity of the Holocaust was revealed at the conclusion of World War Two, much of the Christian world undertook a serious reassessment of their attitudes and teachings concerning the Jewish people. The Nazi slaughter of over six million Jews came as a moral shock to many churches and denominations since they knew their anti-Semitic doctrines had contributed greatly to this horrific crime. Yet that alone did not trigger a change in course, as many Christians could have easily pointed to the Shoah as just further proof that the Jews were divinely cursed for killing Christ. It was the sudden rebirth of the nation of Israel only three years later which proved to be a theological shock to the Christian world, because it seriously challenged the belief that the Jews were cursed to endless wanderings. Thus, the combination of the Holocaust's exposure in 1945 and the rebirth of Israel in 1948 forced many Christian leaders and denominations to revisit their official doctrines and change direction. Thus the Catholic Church, for instance, has formally renounced Replacement theology, recognized the state of Israel, and declared anti-Semitism to be a sin, among other reforms.

Still, anti-Semitism has not disappeared in the post-Holocaust era. Instead it has re-emerged as strong as ever in the form of anti-Zionism or anti-Israelism. Utilizing a warped mixture of religious, racial and conspiratorial anti-Semitism, it largely takes aim today at the collective Jew represented by the revived nation of Israel. The Israeli state is deemed to be inherently evil from the outset for massacring Palestinian Arabs and stealing their land.

Zionism is portrayed as a depraved form of Western colonialism, a crazed expression of religious extremism, and a hateful brand of racial and ethnic bigotry – all wrapped into one. The IDF is accused of being worse than the Nazis. Israel is charged with poisoning Palestinian wells or distributing candy which makes Arabs impotent. Israelis are kidnapping Palestinians to harvest their organs. These are just some of modern-day blood libels against the Jews. The worst practitioners of this contemporary anti-Semitism are in the Arab and Muslim world, which should come as no surprise since many of the top Nazi propagandists found refuge in the Middle East after World War II and brought many of the old lies and blood libels with them.

In essence, this new anti-Semitism seeks to deny the Jewish people the right to a state of their own. In singling out the Jewish state for criticism and censure, and seeking to isolate and remove Israel from the family of nations, anti-Zionism is nothing less than anti-Semitism masquerading under new false pretexts. It is the same old ancient hatred trying to hide behind a new mask, primarily a distorted formulation of international human rights.

The Real Root Of Anti-Semitism

Why has anti-Semitism been able to flourish even into modern times? Because the real root of this malady is spiritual. Ever since God's election of Israel for the purpose of world salvation, Satan has been targeting the Jewish people in order to destroy them and thereby thwart God's redemptive plan. He has done so by sowing the seed of jealousy and rejection against the Chosen people in the nations around Israel. We see it, for instance, in the way Amalek took advantage of the Israelites' weaknesses as they exited Egypt. God warned Israel that there would be similar Amaleks arising in every generation with the intent to destroy Israel (Exodus 17:14-16).

The story of Esther contains one such episode, when Haman – a descendant of Agag the Amalekite (see Esther 3:1 and 1 Samuel 15:32) – accused the Jews of acting superior and plotting against the Persian throne. These were classic expressions of religious, racial and conspiratorial anti-Semitism. Oddly, the Scroll of Esther is the only book in the Bible in which God is never mentioned. He remains a hidden deliverer. Yet right beside this story in our Bibles is the Book of Job, which rolls back the curtain on the spiritual battles underlying events in the natural world. God shows up here quite profoundly, not just as the Creator but also as a very personal God who cares deeply even for one single person. Satan also shows up as the accuser of God's servants.

The lesson is that there is indeed a spiritual battle taking place over the calling and fate of the Jewish people and the restored nation of Israel. We all have a clear choice in this hidden struggle. We can either listen to the demonic voices which seek to slander and ultimately eradicate the Jewish people and nation, or we can honor God's enduring election over Israel for the purpose of redeeming the world. Thankfully, there are millions of Christians today who have become wise to the wiles of the devil and are standing up for Israel and the Jewish people as never before. Just as there is a "mystery" to the irrational hatred of Jews, there also is a mystery to the great love God is planting in the hearts of Christians worldwide for His people Israel. May the Lord give us strength and courage to confront anti-Semitism in all its devious forms in our day.

David Parsons serves as Media and Public Relations Director with the International Christian Embassy Jerusalem. He is also the executive producer of the Front Page Jerusalem radio program and former contributing Christian editor of *The Jerusalem Post Christian Edition.*

CHAPTER THREE

Christians and Jews Together for Israel

JoAnn G. Magnuson

The title for this chapter is "Christians and Jews Together for Israel." However, in order to discuss any togetherness among Christians and Jews, we have to face the fact that it has been a very long time since these two groups have been together in any recognizable sense whatsoever. While we won't have time to discuss the history of Christian-Jewish relations here, I will list a few useful resources at the end of this chapter. We cannot appreciate the recent beginnings of "togetherness" without reminding ourselves of the issues that caused the "apartness."

I am an Evangelical Christian with a life-long interest in the relationship between Christians and Jews. I grew up in a Jewish neighborhood and have been blessed with a long list of Jewish friends. Over a lifetime of Bible reading, I have been impressed with the amount of space given in the sacred text to our father Abraham, his family, their relationship with God, and the attention paid to the details of their connection to a small strip of land along the eastern coast of the Mediterranean Sea.

The long-term relationship of the Jewish people to their ancient homeland is a major theme in scripture and is often referred to as "Zionism." There are many aspects of this concept, but let's try to define "mere" Zionism, the most basic notion of Zionism that seems to be suggested in the Bible.

The term Zionism was coined in 1891 by the Austrian publicist Nathan Birnbaum. A Zionist is anyone who believes the Jews have a right to return to their ancient homeland. Birnbaum played a prominent part in the First Zionist Congress (1897) where Theodor Herzl called for the founding of a Jewish State.

Zionism supports the return of the Jewish people to Zion, to the land of Israel, to the land promised by God to Abraham and his descendants forever. This promise appears often in scripture, but we find the first reference in Genesis 12:1-3. It is enlarged upon by Genesis 15:7: "God said unto Abraham, I am the Lord who brought you out of the land of Ur of the Chaldees to give this land to you to inherit it."

> **The term Zionism was coined in 1891 by the Austrian publicist Nathan Birnbaum. A Zionist is anyone who believes the Jews have a right to return to their ancient homeland.**

If Zionism is the support of the return of the Jewish people to the land of Israel, Christian Zionism is simply Christian support for the return of the Jewish people to the land of Israel. Not every Christian who cares about the Jewish people wants to be called a Christian Zionist, and the terminology is not crucial. Our real question is, where should Christians see the Jews fitting into God's ongoing plan for the world? Is there still a place for the Jews as God's covenant people? If so, how should Christians relate to their Jewish neighbors?

Background of Jewish-Christian Relations

A doctrine, later known as "supersessionism" and sometimes referred to as "replacement theology," appeared early in Church history and has complicated Jewish-Christian relations ever since. As the Church moved away from Israel and its Jewish matrix, Christian theologians began to see Christianity not just as an extension but as a replacement of Israel.

Most of the earliest Christians were Jewish, but the church gradually lost interest in its Jewish roots and heritage as it moved into the pagan world. While there was certainly some persecution of the early Christians by the official Jewish leadership, most Christians in the first generations saw themselves as Jews. By the third century C.E., however, few Christians thought of Jesus as a Jewish teacher or rabbi. Still fewer thought of God's prophets, priests, kings, and apostles as Jews. Some medieval Christian pilgrims remembered the ancient, biblical Jews while traveling to the Holy Land, but few felt connected to the contemporary Jews they met along the way.

By the fourth century the accepted view was that the Church had totally replaced Israel and the Jewish people as a carrier of God's covenant. This view prevailed, with few dissenting voices, until the dawn of the Reformation period. As ordinary people began to have access to the Bible in their own languages, many readers noticed a fairly obvious fact: much space in the sacred text is given to the relationship between God and the land and the people of Israel. This led many Christian readers of the Bible to conclude that God intended the Jewish people to come back to their ancient land in the latter days of human history. This view is sometimes called "Restorationism," and in recent times has been known as Christian Zionism.

The word "restore" implies the act of giving something back that has been lost or stolen, a return to a former or a normal condition. Isaiah tells us to "Look to the rock from which you were cut and to the quarry from which you were hewn; look to Abraham, your father, and to Sarah, who gave you birth..." (Isaiah 51:1-2). The Christian church has neglected her relationship with our spiritual parents, Abraham and Sarah, their descendants and their worldview for so long that it has been nearly lost and mostly forgotten.

As we have noted, early in Christian history, as church leadership moved away from the land of Israel, many began to ignore, and in some cases to despise the biblical storehouse which contained the Hebraic treasures of our faith. The Old Testament was part of the canon, but it was viewed through a very Christian filter.

I am not suggesting that the effort of the Church Fathers to bring Christian understanding to the Jewish texts was totally wrong and misguided. New ideas and understandings often cause pendulum swings in history. However, this particular swing has had some very unfortunate side effects.

Restoration Efforts

There have been several points in history when Christians endeavored to restore their connection to their Hebrew heritage. A fascinating account of various Christian efforts to discover the quarry from which we Christians were hewn is found in Barbara Tuchman's **Bible and Sword: England and Palestine from the Bronze Age to Balfour**. This book traces the path of an interesting assortment of Christians who, for one reason or another, looked to the quarry from which they were hewn, to the olive tree into which they were grafted (Romans 11:17-21).

> **There have been several points in history when Christians endeavored to restore their connection to their Hebrew heritage.**

Studying the history of those who believed that the descendants of Abraham, Isaac, and Jacob would return to the land the Lord promised to them is a study in the amazing grace of God — grace because it is quite clear that many of the individuals involved took wrong turns and usually made progress by accident. Radio host and Jewish theologian Dennis Prager refers to Genesis as "an account of the world's first recorded dysfunctional family" (not that we've seen many fully functional families since the angel barred the gate to Eden). In both the Christian and the Jewish branches of the family, the lovers of Zion have been a rather eccentric crew. Tuchman comments on this phenomenon: "It is a curious fact that so many notable English eccentrics have been drawn irresistibly to the East. Perhaps it was because most of them, like T. E. Lawrence, the archetype, were voyaging on some private religious or metaphysical quest of their own and, like Disraeli's Tancred, sought spiritual rebirth in the place where three great religions were conceived." Or perhaps it is simply that those seeking God, however confused their motives, tended to search in the land where it all began.

As history continued, anti-Semitism became quite well entrenched in Christian thought. We modern Christians need to study this history in order to understand why Jews often fear Christians in positions of power. I have spent much of my adult life teaching about the history of anti-Semitism and the Holocaust. Until Christian educators take seriously the stains on our own historical record, we should not be surprised that our efforts at building togetherness still make many of our Jewish neighbors nervous. We must not send our young Christians off to college ignorant of the anti-Jewish writings of the Church Fathers, the Crusades, the Inquisition, and the social climate in Christian Europe that allowed the Nazis to come to power.

Since World War II, as the shocking details of the Holocaust became public knowledge, some Church leaders began to wake up to the damage caused by theological anti-Semitism. In the post-war years, significant progress has been made in Jewish-Christian relations. The birth of modern Israel has given the Jewish people a home base in which to rebuild after centuries in dispersion. This homeland has also given Jews and Christians the opportunity to meet together and to encounter each other as equal partners in the study of, among other things, archeology, geography, history, biblical languages and biblical texts.

The ensuing dialogue has been rich. Catholic scholars deserve a great deal of credit for this movement. The Second Vatican Council was instrumental in producing the document called Nostra Aetate, "In Our Time." This led to many positive changes within Catholic circles concerning their relationship with the Jewish community. Individually, Catholic leaders such as Sister Rose Thering and Father Edward Flannery led the movement toward dialogue with the Jewish community in the United States.

Current State of Togetherness

Evangelical Christians showed less interest in Jewish-Christian dialogue in the early post-war years. We Evangelicals have generally been better at proclamation than at dialogue. There was a mixture of opinion in the Evangelical world after the founding of the state of Israel in 1948. Some believed that the restoration of Israel was a fulfillment of biblical prophecy, while others questioned such a view. After the 1967 Six-Day War and the reunification of Jerusalem under Israeli control, more Evangelicals became actively supportive of Israel. Organizations such as the International Christian Embassy, Jerusalem (ICEJ); Bridges for Peace; Christian Friends of Israel; National Christian Leadership Conference for Israel and the International Fellowship of Christians and Jews, all sprang up during the 1970s and 1980s. The movement now often identified as Christian Zionism began to gain traction in the Evangelical world.

I would like to suggest that there is a linkage between two Christian movements that developed in the second half of the 20th century: the Charismatic Renewal and Christian Zionism. While the Charismatic renewal is known for its rediscovery of the more exotic spiritual gifts, I suggest that the renewal's most enduring contribution was getting Christians from liturgical backgrounds to read the Bible from Genesis to Revelation. Many folks in these churches knew only the parts of the Bible that they heard as assigned readings on specific Sundays. As Catholics and mainline Protestants began to associate with Evangelicals and Pentecostals and read the Bible together, Christians began to appreciate one another and they also discovered the importance of the Jews in God's eternal plan.

In the 1970s and '80s groups of Christians who were interested in Israel began to hold conferences and go on Israel tours. There were, of course, many pro-Israel Christian individuals who had been working in the field from the early years of the Reformation, but groups of Christians reaching out to Jews, with motives other than converting them, really begins in this period.

Most of the organizations in these early years were headquartered in Israel. This was important at this point because Christians whose interest in Israel was based on biblical sources needed to see modern Israel and meet contemporary Jewish people. Since we hadn't really talked to each other for nearly 2000 years, we needed some time to get reacquainted. Togetherness happened occasionally when large groups of Christians – for instance the ICEJ's annual Feast of Tabernacles event – invited a few Jewish speakers to address them, or when large Jewish groups ¬– like the American Israel Public Affairs Committee (AIPAC) invited a few Christians to speak. When I first joined AIPAC in 1981 I think there were about 15 Christians in attendance. There were over 400 in 2016.

The first time that I recall being in a meeting where there were somewhat equal numbers of Jews and Christians was when my Kansas City Jewish friend, Esther Levens, began Voices United for Israel in 1991. Esther's husband had been a long-time AIPAC activist and after he died Esther began a search for Christian partners. She had read polling data indicating that a majority of American Christians supported Israel and she decided that Jews and Christians needed to know each other better. She gathered a small group of Jews and Christians together after an AIPAC meeting and began a group that eventually included about 200 organizations – from both communities. Esther knew David Bar-Illan, Prime Minister Netanyahu's Director of Communications, and we began a continuing cycle of meetings on Capitol Hill where various Israelis and American Jews participated in seminars for members of Congress.

In 2006 a new U.S. Christian organization supporting Israel was born. **Christians United for Israel (CUFI)** was founded by Rev. John Hagee. This was an important step forward. Although the Jerusalem-based Christian groups filled a major vacuum, we needed a U.S. entity to have influence on American policy and relationship building. CUFI's annual Washington D.C. Summit is modeled after AIPAC's annual Policy Conference. Both groups now bring large delegations of American citizens to the nation's capitol to present their views to their elected officials. Having both Christians and Jews in leadership roles is, I believe, one of CUFI's strengths. David Brog, CUFI's Jewish Executive Director, has written several books and many articles on topics relating to Jewish-Christian history and relationships. He has brought much wisdom to our collective table.

One area the Christian Zionist community needs to develop is the building of local activities. It is great to go to Washington and Jerusalem to attend conferences and hear great speakers, but the goal of those activities should be to build relationships back home. My hometown, Minneapolis, Minnesota, was for many years known as the most anti-Semitic city in North America. Many good people have played roles in changing that status. I will mention two of them. Hubert Humphrey, mayor of Minneapolis in the late 1940s, brought Jews into his city government. G. Douglas Young, a Bible scholar who came to Minneapolis in 1951 to teach at Northwestern Bible College, reached out to the Jewish community. Dr. Young was a passionate Christian Zionist and was very concerned about the newly created State of Israel.

He brought news about Israel to his weekly Christian radio broadcast. He and his wife moved to Israel in the early 1960s and founded the Institute of Holy Land Studies in Jerusalem, where students from various Christian backgrounds could spend time learning from Jewish and Christian teachers in the land of the Bible. Many of those students are leaders of Christian Zionist groups today. Dr. Young's favorable reputation with the local Jewish community blazed a trail I was privileged to follow in the years to come.

With the help of several friendly local churches, a group of friends and I have been able to host regular meetings to teach about Israel and to meet with members of the local Jewish community. We've done this on a more or less regular basis for at least 40 years now. When I suggest to people that starting new groups that meet monthly, or at least quarterly, meetings are important, I am often told, "Oh but we don't have a budget for that." My response is that if you have access to a room that you can heat in the winter and cool in the summer; a stash of folding chairs; a screen or a blank wall where you can show films and PowerPoint teachings and a coffee pot – you'll be set to start local meetings. If you want help, email me at jgmagnuson@mac.com and I'll send you a list of good films, suggested reading lists and other ideas that have worked here.

Congressman Tip O'Neill used to say, "All politics is local." I firmly believe that all worthwhile causes are local too. Reach out to your local Jewish community. People who know each other are more likely to help each other when the going gets tough.

Suggested Reading:

Why The Jews? The Reason for Anti-Semitism
Dennis Prager & Joseph Telushkin, Simon & Schuster.
One of the best books on the subject. Well-documented research.

Antisemitism and the Jewish Experience
A Brief Introduction for Christians
40 page booklet with basic information
JoAnn G. Magnuson, self-published

Bible and Sword: England and Palestine from the Bronze Age to Balfour
Barbara Tuchman, Post-biblical history, New York: Minerva, 1968

JoAnne Magnuson serves as the Curator for the Jewish-Christian Library Centers. She is also the author of the book, *Antisemitism and the Jewish Experience.*

CHAPTER FOUR

Who's Land?

Steve Coplon

Putting Things in Perspective

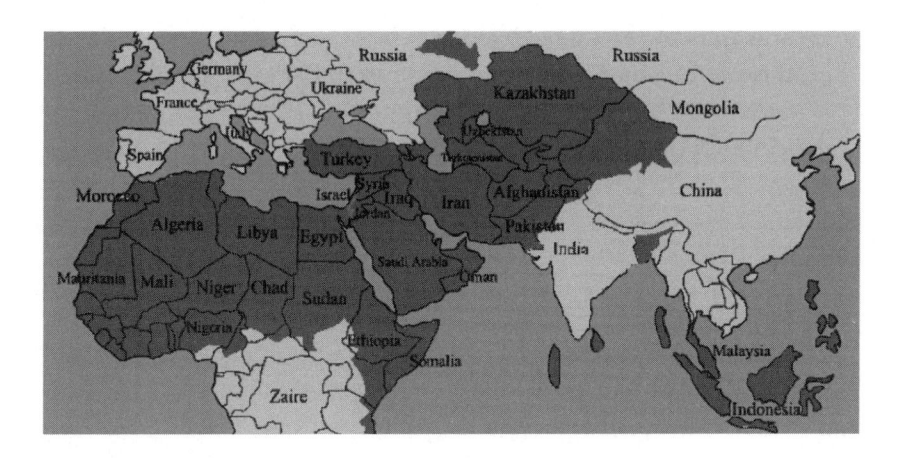

The one Jewish State of Israel with 8.5 million people (20% of whom are Arab) dwells amidst dozens of Muslim nations with nearly 200 times as many people and several thousand times more land than the single Jewish State. Since her birth on May 14, 1948, every day is an existential day of survival for the Jewish State as many would seek to occupy Israel and drive them into the sea.

Epidemic of Terrorism

Thousands of Jews have been killed by terrorists since 1948, and for over a hundred years, the Jews in the land (before and after the birth of Israel) have been victims of a steady stream of violence and terror. Whether it was the Arab riots of the 1920's or the 1936 riots, the aim was to terrorize the Jews in the Promised Land. Hundreds were killed and many more wounded. After the birth of Israel, the Israelis were subject to a long period of terror from 1949-1952. In the late 50s and early 60s the newly formed PLO began to use terror. These tactics ultimately turned into plane hijackings, bombings, massacres and more. Even after peace agreements began to emerge in the 1970s, 80s, and 90s terrorism rose with the Intifada, suicide bombers, rockets, and random stabbings, and more. The killing of innocent civilians, such as the 13-year-old-girl killed recently is the latest evidence of a savagery motivated not by the love of peace but a deeply rooted hatred for the Jewish people. No good will, no olive branch, no agreement has been able to abate decades of violence, terror, and murder. Amidst this environment Israel seeks to have peace and a two state solution.

Thousands of Jews have been killed by terrorists since 1948, and for over a hundred years, the Jews in the land (before and after the birth of Israel) have been victims of a steady stream of violence and terror.

Missiles Galore

In addition, Israel has over 120,000 missiles aimed at all of her population centers (some experts say as many as 200,000). Nearly all of these missiles are just minutes away (some are seconds away) from Israel. Southern Lebanon and Gaza have the vast majority of these missiles. Both of these lands were returned for the sake of peace and now are the launching pads for terror and war. Since 2005, over 25,000 rockets have been fired into Israel from the lands that Israel returned to its inhabitants. This has led to ongoing Israeli intervention to root out these missiles and their launching sites. Hamas and Hezbollah, two Islamic terror groups control these lands and have no plans for peace. Their stated goal is the destruction of Israel. Amazingly, they have hidden many missiles and launching sites in hospitals, schools and other places in which children and the infirm reside or congregate. In 1957, Golda Meir said, "Peace will come when the Arabs will love their children more than they hate us." Sadly, little has changed during the past 60 years.

Israel Not Without Faults

Israel's values are rooted in the Torah. Thus, Israel has had so much in common with Judeo-Christian nations. This is why Israel is passionate about the standards of justice it must uphold. At the same time, Israel is not without flaws, flaws common to all of civilization. There have been instances of government corruption. During war, Israel has killed civilians (nearly always accidentally). A check point disruption caused a healthcare delay leading to a bad medical outcome for a Palestinian. On occasion, Israeli soldiers have unjustly harassed citizens and non-citizens. There have been instances of discrimination. A young American woman was accidentally killed by a bulldozer as she protested Israel's presence in Gaza.

Yet with certainty, when adverse events occur, they are outliers and not mainstream events. They are rarely pre-meditated and almost always addressed with appropriate actions of justice by the Israelis toward the Israelis who are responsible. For example, former President Katsav was found guilty of rape. His case was overseen by an Arab-Israeli judge. He was sentenced to prison. Inquiries and discipline have occurred to soldiers who step outside the scope of their mission and orders.

In spite of her faults, there is no ground for the doctrine of moral equivalence between Israel and her neighbors. Israel is the only free country in the region and the only country seeking to ensure an ongoing expansion of liberty. If one has any doubts, compare the status of women in Israel juxtaposed to Israel's neighbors. The Islamic policy of wife-beating, the grotesque practice of genital mutilation, as well as the practice of a man having multiple wives shows that women are generally less than second class citizens in most of the Muslim nations.

On the Other Hand

Over 20% of the Israel's citizens are Arabs (most of whom are Muslims). These citizens have all the same rights as Jews. They can serve in the Knesset (and do); they can serve on the Supreme Court (and do); they can vote in elections (and do); they can serve in the army (and do). They even have been athletes representing Israel and contestants who have won the Miss Israel pageant. All Israeli citizens (Jew and Arab and other) have the opportunity to succeed in Israel – politically, economically, socially, and otherwise. The bottom line is that the Arab citizens of Israel have more rights in the Jewish State than they would have in any of the Arab or Muslim states. No wonder they choose to stay.

Over 3,000 Years of Uninterrupted Jewish Presence

Jews have inhabited the Promised Land – without interruption – for over 3,000 years. Even during the darkest hours of Jewish history, a remnant of Jews remained in the land. Thus, there is no rightful claim to the land other than by those to whom it was given over 3,000 years ago and who have possessed it in all or in part for every day of the past 3,000+ years.

Only a Jewish Independent State Has Existed in the Land

In the history of the world, only three independent states have ever existed in the Promised Land. All three of these states were Jewish States. The first of these was the land possessed by Joshua and later ruled by Judges and then the kings. The second state was the nation recovered after the Babylonian captivity under Zerubbabel and later Nehemiah and others. This nation ceased existing around the year 73 A.D. The third state is the modern State of Israel born on May 14, 1948. All three of these nations were Jewish states.

During the gaps of Israeli sovereignty – during the Babylonian Captivity of 70 years – during the nearly 1,900 years of diaspora from the 1st century to the 20th century – no nation, no people claimed the Promised Land as its homeland. Through it all, some Jews remained in the land. When the Jews in diaspora sought to return to their land there was fierce opposition – political, philosophical, military, and other to prevent and oppose the land's possessors to restore their national homeland as a state.

The Modern State of Israel – Born Through International Law

The birth of the modern State of Israel is unquestionably a miracle of God's grace. The nation was being conceived in the hearts of many who longed for Zion. Simultaneously, some in authority found pathways of international law to establish the Jewish State. In 1917, Lord Balfour of Britain wrote a declaration "viewing with favor a national home for the Jewish people."

The contents of the declaration are as follows:

Foreign Office – November 2, 1917

Dear Lord Rothschild:

I have much pleasure in conveying to you, on behalf of His Majesty's Government, the following declaration of sympathy with Jewish Zionist aspirations which has been submitted to and approved by the Cabinet.

'His Majesty's Government views with favor the establishment in Palestine of a national home for the Jewish people, and will use their best endeavors to facilitate the achievement of this object, it being clearly understood that nothing shall be done which may prejudice the civil and religious rights of existing non-Jewish communities in Palestine or the rights and political status enjoyed by Jews in any other country.'

I should be grateful if you would bring this declaration to the knowledge of the Zionist Federation.

Signed – Lord Balfour

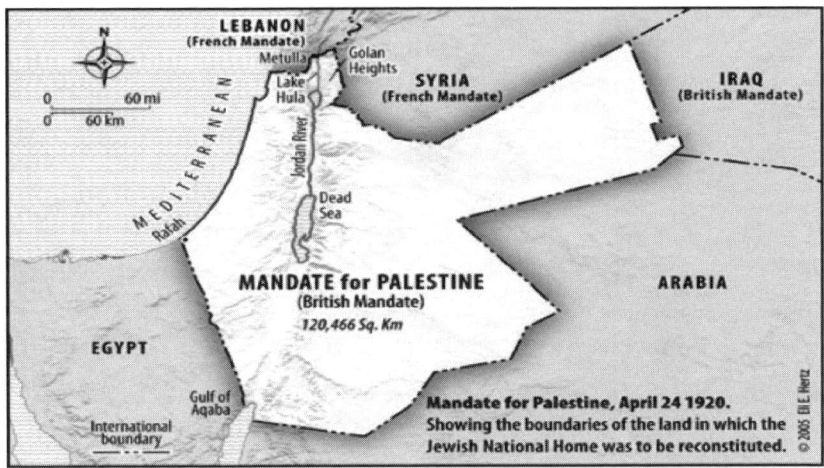

Mandate for Palestine, April 24 1920. Showing the boundaries of the land in which the Jewish National Home was to be reconstituted.

Three years later, in 1920, the San Remo Conference convened and identified the mandate for Palestine – the provision of land assured for a Jewish National Homeland. Notice the size of the land under this plan. It contains all of the modern state of Israel (including Gaza, the Golan, The West Bank, plus Jordan.

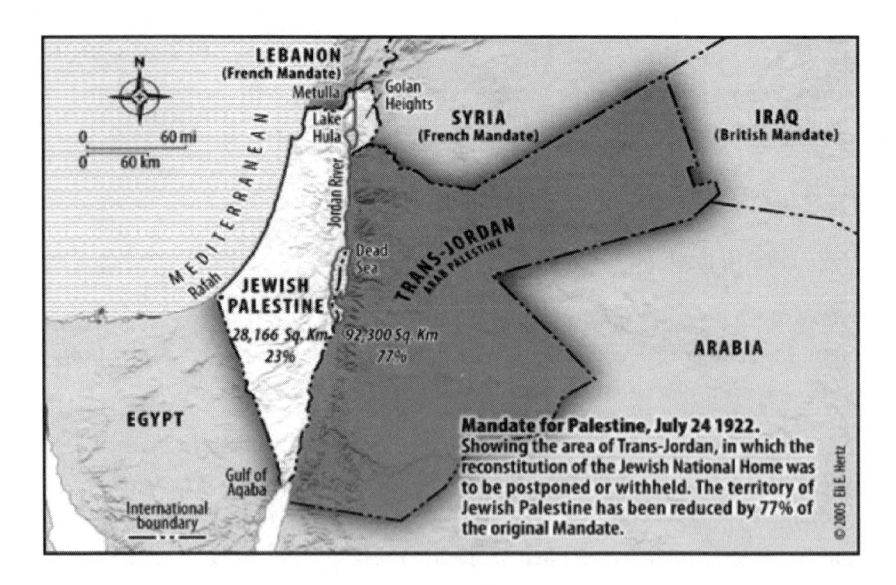

Mandate for Palestine, July 24 1922. Showing the area of Trans-Jordan, in which the reconstitution of the Jewish National Home was to be postponed or withheld. The territory of Jewish Palestine has been reduced by 77% of the original Mandate.

In 1922, the League of Nations voted 51-0 to approve the land called Jewish Palestine for a national homeland for the Jews. This land is roughly the equivalent to the land currently possessed by Israel + the land dwelt in by "Palestinians" on the "West Bank" and Gaza. It is 23% of the allocation from the 1920 plan. The remaining 77% is called Transjordan for the Arabs.

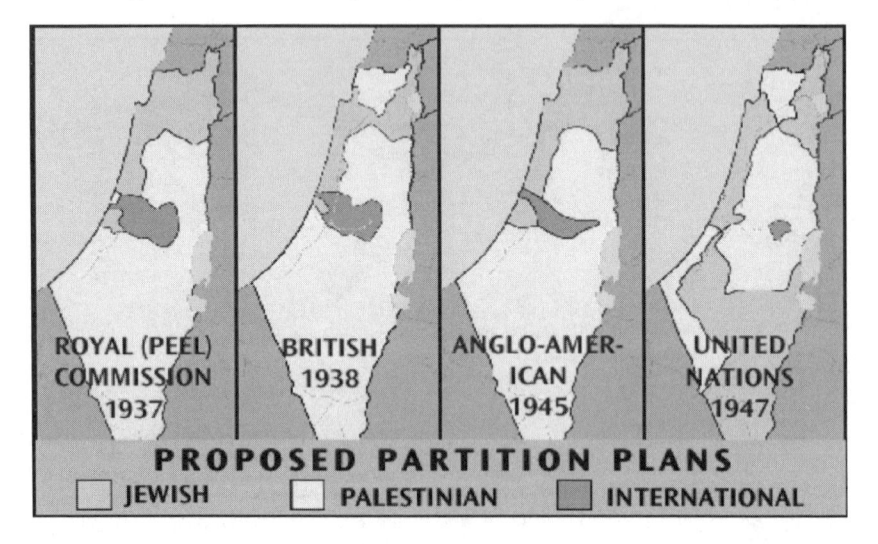

PROPOSED PARTITION PLANS
ROYAL (PEEL) COMMISSION 1937 | BRITISH 1938 | ANGLO-AMERICAN 1945 | UNITED NATIONS 1947

☐ JEWISH ☐ PALESTINIAN ■ INTERNATIONAL

In the 1930s three commissions put their approval upon a land for the Jewish people – with each carving up the 1922 plan into smaller pieces. By the time the UN Partition plan of 1947 emerged, the allocated land was less than 12% of the original mandate. All of the Arab nations walked out refusing the internationally recognized partition plan.

In November of 1947 this plan was approved 33-13 by the United Nations – a watershed moment in history. With UN recognition came preparation for national declaration, with significant world approval.

Six months later on May 14, 1948 the modern State of Israel was born. Within one hour the United States recognized the new state. The Soviet Union followed suit. Within a few hours war ensued as seven armies from surrounding Arab nations invaded Israel seeking to totally destroy her. Against all odds, Israel prevailed.

One Side Wants the Other Side Dead

Since 1948, a significant number of Israel's neighbors have wanted Israel destroyed (as evidenced by 10 wars and endless terrorism). Nearly every six years, Israel has prosecuted a war for its very existence or a war that threatened a large percentage of its population. "The truth is that if Israel were to put down its arms there would be no more Israel. If the Arabs were to put down their arms there would be no more war." (Benjamin Netanyahu)

Refugee Reality

During the period of statehood and the war for independence over 850,000 Jews were displaced as they were banished from their homes throughout the Middle East and North Africa. At the same time about 600,000 Arab refugees fled the newly formed State of Israel waiting for their Arab brethren to drive the Jews into the sea. The newly formed Jewish state incorporated the 850,000 refugees. The surrounding Arab nations did not, intentionally producing the crisis of the displaced "Palestinian" people, a crisis that remains to this day.

Ralph Galloway, former head of the United Nations Relief and Works Agency for Palestinian Refugees said, "The Arab States do not want to solve the refugee problem. They want to keep it as an open sore, as an affront to the United Nations and as a weapon against Israel.

Two State Solutions – A Summary

At least a half-dozen two state solution proposals were proffered prior to 1948. All of these were accepted by the Jews and rejected by the Arabs. Since that time numerous additional two state solutions have been accepted by Israel and rejected by the "Palestinians" (the Arabs). The pressure to solve this problem accelerated after the Six Day War, when Jordan lost the "West Bank" to Israel

Before and After the Six Day War

In June, 1967, several armies perched on Israel's borders, ready to invade. Israel won a remarkable preemptive victory. In the process, the entire Sinai, Gaza, and Judea and Samaria came under Israeli control. Former terrorist (who converted to Christ) Wahid Shoebat said, "One day I was a Jordanian, the next day a Palestinian." This was part of a new strategy to vilify Israel for "refugees" in "occupied lands" resulting from war. It also became the excuse for dozens of acts of Palestinian terror such as the Munich Massacre at the 1972 Olympics.

Palestine and Palestinians

The origin of the name Palestine was determined by the Romans in the year 135 A.D. after crushing the Bar Kokhba rebellion. All who lived in the region resided in Syria Palestinia, whether Jews or non-Jews. In the 19th and 20th centuries Jews and non-Jews lived in a land called Palestine. When the State of Israel was born it was headlined in The Palestine Post (now called the Jerusalem Post). In reality, a Palestinian is a term of the past – but it never referred to a specific people but to any and all inhabitants of the land – Jew or non-Jew. From 135 A.D. to 1948 there were both Jewish Palestinians and non-Jewish Palestinians. Today there is a nation called Israel. In Israel there are Jewish and non-Jewish residents (citizens). Meanwhile the lands of Judea and Samaria are inhabited by 1.7 million Arabs with no citizenship (formerly of Jordan) while the two million Arabs in Israel have full rights as citizens of Israel. Israel has offered both pathways to citizenship and pathways to statehood. These are rejected over and over and over again.

What About Occupied Territories?

The present "occupied" lands were possessed for national security reasons during the time of war. Israel willingly submitted to an international effort to draft documents for peace and the potential return of "territories." The language of that document specifically mentioned the general term "territories" and not "all territories" or "the territories" since the writers assumed there a buffer needed to maintain the peace. The Arab nations rejected all offers for negotiation of return of territories. The "Palestinians" have followed suit – over and over and over again.

Israel has offered to return 95% or more of the land on several occasions. Each time the offer was rejected and usually the rejection was followed by terror from the intifada or suicide bombers or rockets or a combination of these.

Land for Peace

Israel has proven that land for peace is possible. In 1979 Israel and Egypt completed the historic Camp David Accords. Under the agreement Israel systematically returned the Sinai to Egypt in return for peace. The Sinai is three times the size of the State of Israel – giving evidence of the willingness of Israel to give up large tracts of land. This agreement has held firm for over 35 years. Israel also entered into an agreement with Jordan in 1994. This agreement brought the two countries closer together to work to maintain the peace between them as they share a common border and common interests. Since the agreement, travel and commerce between the two countries has greatly increased.

Land for War

In 1993, Israel and the Palestinian Authority (PA) consummated the Oslo Accords. Within a year, Israel began withdrawing from regions of Judea and Samaria including Jericho and then Hebron. Almost immediately, the Palestinians began desecrating holy Jewish sites such as the tombs of the patriarchs in Hebron.

Meanwhile, The PA was able to establish its headquarters, a government, a security force, and more. Israel then agreed to discuss the final status of the lands including Jerusalem. In the end, there was significant conflict as another intifada occurred and then suicide bombers began blowing up buses, restaurants, and other establishments killing multitudes of people. To the Palestinian leadership it is land for war, all part of the Hamas strategy on incremental destruction of Israel. Israel withdrew from Southern Lebanon in 2000. In return, thousands of rockets have rained down upon Israel. Hezbollah, funded primarily by Iran, is behind this campaign of terror. With Hezbollah, it is land for war.

In 2006, Israel withdrew from Gaza. War hero, General and Prime Minister, Ariel Sharon oversaw the withdrawal. In return there has been continuous conflict. This includes thousands of missiles fired into Israel. In the meantime, Israel ensures that tons of supplies make it into Gaza each week. These are a lifeline to the people of Gaza. Tragically, many of the construction supplies were used to build terror tunnels and other means of war. Whenever Israel has retaliated to eliminate the terror tunnels or missiles, it gives ample warning to the residents of Gaza to vacate those areas. This is remarkable! With Hamas in charge of Gaza, it is land for war, the people of Gaza deprived of basic necessities.

The question remains, with the withdrawal from Lebanon, the withdrawal from Gaza, the withdrawals from Judea and Samaria, why is Israel the primary recipient of blame, vitriol, and hatred? What nation would receive tens of thousands of rockets fired on its territory and conduct a measured response? Who will speak up for those in Gaza and Southern Lebanon and ask why is their leadership conducting a war machine rather than taking care of their people in the territories ceded to them by Israel?

No, No, a Thousand Times No!

For a hundred years the Arabs had rejected agreement after agreement for the final status of a two state solution. Whether it was the rejection of the Balfour declaration in 1917, the San Remo Conference in 1920, the Peel Commission in 1937, The United Nations in 1947, and dozens of proposals before and since, there has been one consistent unilateral position by the Arabs and Palestinians – No! After the 1967 Six Day War, the public proclamation made in Khartoum on September 1, 1967 was very simple and very telling:

"No Peace with Israel, No Recognition of Israel, No Negotiation with Israel"

Since this dictum the Palestinians have continually rejected various proposals for a two-state solution. From 1993 to the present hour numerous similar proposals have been offered, all of them were rejected – usually followed by a wave of terror against Israeli citizens. In 2000, the PA received an offer, by Israeli PM Barak. This proposal returned over 95% of "The West Bank", East Jerusalem, all of Gaza, and a small percentage of Israel. This proposal, like every other was met with a resounding, "No." President Clinton, Ambassador Dennis Ross, and Secretary of State Albright were astounded by the rejection by Arafat and the PA. They all say that Arafat blew his best chance for peace. The rejection demonstrates that it is not Israel who is occupying it is the Palestinians who are stonewalling – as part of an overall strategy to demonize, demoralize, and destroy Israel.

Given the many rejected opportunities for peace agreements, former Israeli Foreign Minister Abba Eban said, "The Arabs never miss an opportunity to miss an opportunity."

Statehood Rejected

There have been numerous opportunities for a reasonable two-state solution. In every instance, Israel has said yes while the Arab (Palestinian) contingent has said no. Prime Minister Rabin offered statehood, it was rejected. Prime Minister Netanyahu offered statehood, it was rejected. Prime Minister Barak offered statehood, it was rejected. Prime Minister Sharon made many overtures for statehood, they were rebuffed. Prime Minister Olmert offered statehood, it was rejected. Prime Minister Netanyahu is willing to negotiate and continues to be rebuffed.

Palestinian Rights Misnomers

The Nonsense of Genocide: Israel is accused of Genocide.
Here are the facts:
- There are more Arabs in Israel than there were in 1948 – case closed.

- It is the Jews who face the existential threat of suicide from 120,000 rockets and missiles, advanced armies, and a potential nuclear armed Iran – case closed.

- When Israel removes the missiles or launchers, it provides ample notice to those who reside in that area to vacate their premises; hardly an act of genocide – case closed.

- The false charge of genocide is a crime of the highest proportions.

-

The Nonsense of Apartheid: Israel is falsely accused of Apartheid.
Here are the facts:
- Over 100,000 Palestinians travel into Israel every day to work at better paying jobs (average wage is more than double) – case closed. The security fence has done its job – bringing a virtual end to the suicide bombers while letting visitors, workers, and commerce continue flowing – case closed.

- It is the Palestinian leadership that has squandered billions in aid for the Palestinian people – facilitating the state of squalor for many – case closed.

- There is no racial segregation (the definition of Apartheid), only an offer of statehood summarily rejected multiple times by Arafat, Abbas, and the leadership of the Palestinian Authority – case closed.

- Every day multitudes of "Palestinians" receive world-class medical care inside Israeli hospitals and medical facilities

- Every day, tons of supplies and provisions are trucked into various "Palestinian" territories.

Conclusion

Regarding the assertion that "Israel is an evil occupier" the words of Daniel Patrick Moynihan ring adroitly true, "You are entitled to your own opinions, but you are not entitled to your own facts." Bottom line – there is not a shred of evidence that Israel is an evil occupier – rather, it is the only outpost of hope and freedom and opportunity in the Middle East – even for Arabs – living under a constant existential threat from multiple enemies. Amidst the vitriol, threats, and horrific violence Israel has exercised remarkable restraint in dealing with enemies committed to her destruction. Israel has ceded huge tracts of land – The Sinai, Gaza, Southern Lebanon, Jericho, Hebron, and more. Meanwhile many magnanimous offers for Palestinian statehood have been proffered. Every offer has been rejected.

It is obvious that the refusal of statehood is designed to keep the false "Evil Occupier" narrative going while Hamas, Hezbollah, the PA, Fatah, Iran and others seek Israel's destruction.

The difference between the two parties is best conveyed by this quote: "When peace comes we will perhaps in time be able to forgive the Arabs for killing our sons, but it will be harder for us to forgive them for having forced us to kill their sons."   Golda Meir

The spiritual individual is able to discern good from evil when they see it (Hebrews 6). Others create their own opinions based upon the manufacture of mythical facts fabricating narratives that neither are nor ever were. In the end the Word of God has the final say:

"Hear the word of the Lord, O nations, and declare it in the isles afar off, and say, 'He who scattered Israel will gather him, and keep him as a shepherd does his flock.' For the Lord has redeemed Jacob, and ransomed him from the hand of one stronger than he. Therefore, they shall come and sing in the height of Zion, streaming to the goodness of the Lord." Jeremiah 31:10-12.

Steve Coplon serves as a board member with Memphis Friends of Israel. This chapter was written with the support of ideas from Dr. Michael Brown.

CHAPTER FIVE

Four Incredibly Important American Blessings to Israel

Edward Holliday

Three unique American blessings bequeathed on the modern nation of Israel have been extraordinarily instrumental to the Jewish state's very existence. A fourth American blessing by a Nobel Peace Prize winner has forever tied Israel to the blessings of freedom. It's impossible to contemplate what might have happened if these American blessings for Israel had not unfolded in the timely manner that they did. Each blessing is a gift that keeps on giving in the life of the modern state of Israel.

The first American blessing came even before Israeli independence happened in 1948. In the time after World War II, and leading up to their independence, the Jews who had lived in the Palestine area for centuries, were joined by Jews from around the world-- especially those displaced from the Nazi atrocities and Holocaust camps in Europe. Since the end of World War I the land of the Bible had been under British control, but a withdrawal date was fixed. The Arabs had already declared that they would not allow a Jewish state to be formed. Many Arab leaders promised to drive the Jews into the Mediterranean Sea if they attempted to re-birth a nation that the world had not seen since the Romans had destroyed Jerusalem and dispersed the Jewish people almost 2,000 years ago.

The odds for survival of a Jewish state in the Middle East were small looking at the numbers. 50,000,000 Arabs to 500,000 Jews were not good numbers. Some Muslims stated that with 50 million, even if they lost 10 million, the war would be worth it. The Jewish communities were separated with no central command structure and very few arms, and virtually no trucks, tanks, or airplanes. Few Jews there had ever had formal military training. Recognizing the poor conditions to fight for survival in a military conflict the Jews sent a personal recruiter to New York. They wanted to convince a Jewish American World War II veteran that his people needed him.

Mickey Marcus was no ordinary soldier. As an attorney, he spent a lot of time in the Pentagon behind a desk, but he savored to be in the fight. He knew military bureaucracy and how to maneuver through it enough to get on a plane and parachute into enemy territory on D-Day. He won medals for valor and knew how to organize. After some reluctance he accepted the challenge to organize the assortment of hodge-podge soldiers who were willing to fight for a new nation. Using his military contacts to influence in the White House to acknowledge the new nation upon declaring independence and attempting to provide equipment for the defense of a new nation, Mickey Marcus came into the land of the Bible at a crucial time.

Like any new arrival, there was resistance to this American who came into the future nation of Israel and tried to bring about a unified command and control structure. He wrote military training manuals by memory, conducted drills, and supervised the development of a fighting force. He was a part of strategic planning sessions and rose to the rank of aluf----the same Hebrew term used for the ancient warrior Joshua who led the Israeli forces into the Battle of Jericho!

Mickey Marcus had his handprints on every aspect of the fledgling Israeli military and when independence was declared Israel fought. The world anticipated a Jewish slaughter, but Mickey Marcus taught the forces to not just defend but to attack and win. Against all odds and against his military training instinct, in one the most lasting flashes of brilliance that helped make Israel what it is today, Marcus saved Jerusalem. The Jewish population in Jerusalem was trapped and starving. The Arab forces had cut off the road leading to the mountainous ancient city. Many Israeli troops died trying to break through. A United Nations brokered cease-fire was to go into effect in a few days. If Israel did not control land in Jerusalem then they would have no claim to any part of its old capital. The political leaders told Mickey Marcus that Israel could not be Israel without Jerusalem. Marcus told them to leave it and accept a country without it. No, was the answer. How would Mickey get through the Arab army blocking the city? Using his uncanny intelligence, Mickey used bulldozers and in an incredible feat of daring and deception he actually built a new road to Jerusalem! The city's Jewish population was saved and the Jews could claim a part of their ancient capital as the U.N. brokered cease-fire went into effect.

Mickey Marcus was the first Israeli general since the Maccabees. He would not personally receive the praise for all his actions because he was also the last casualty before the United Nation's cease-fire. He is buried at West Point where his marker says he was a soldier for all humanity. Ben-Gurion said that he was our very best. It is fitting that as the citizens and politicians in Israel today go to the Knesset that they use a street named for the American Mickey Marcus - the man who had masterminded the building of a new road to save the Jews in Jerusalem and to ensure the ancient capital of Israel would be a part of the modern state of Israel.

The Second Blessing

The second blessing weaves in a beautiful way with the story of Aluf Mickey Marcus. Because as Marcus was organizing the defense of a soon to be declared nation, President Harry Truman was wrestling with the decision whether to recognize such a nation. As the British mandate ended and British protection of the Jewish citizens was removed the Jewish populations were on their own. Security was an uncertainty but the challenge from the neighboring Arab nations was certain. Recognition by other nations was a necessity for survival and acceptance on the world stage. Recognition by the United States would be a bold statement that this young nation was worthy of respect. Most countries in the world had already announced publicly or through internal messages that they would not be rushing to recognize the Jewish nation. A United Nations plan for a partition, that had previously passed, to give the Jews a chance for statehood, was at this point being pushed for a delay or even a complete rejection. A very comprehensive analysis of the touchy day by day decisions whether the U.S. should recognize the new nation *(and at this point no one even knew what the Jews wanted to name their new state if it became independent)* is well documented in David McCullough's biography Truman. President Truman's Secretary of State, George Marshall, was adamantly opposed to recognition. The entire State Department seemed to push against Truman and wanted the president to wait before recognizing the new state. Even Truman's U.N. Ambassador, Austin went before the United Nations General Assembly and said that the U.S. recommended that the partition plan should be abandoned and the land of Palestine should go under a temporary trusteeship by the United Nations.

McCullough documents that Truman called the State Department officers below Marshall those *"striped pants conspirators."* Truman was furious but in private told Jewish leaders that he would recognize Israel. Truman was teetering with personal disaster because his popularity was at a low 36% and the beloved Marshall might resign. Already many Democrats were whispering that someone else should run for president. But Truman surprised his own State Department and those American representatives at the U.N. when he recognized Israel as it declared its independence.

Israeli leaders and citizens were ecstatic. McCullough writes that, **"When the Chief Rabbi of Israel, Isaac Halevi Herzog, called at the White House, he told Truman, 'God put you in your mother's womb so you would be the instrument to bring the rebirth of Israel after two thousand years."** He reported that as these words were said, President Truman had tears running down his cheeks.

The Third Blessing

The third American blessing comes from the Nobel Peace Prize winner, Dr. Martin Luther King, Jr. Some called Dr. King the black Moses. His leadership in the Civil Rights' movement went hand in hand with his duties as a pastor. Knowing the Old Testament well, he painted a picture for the world to see that in many ways his struggle to breakthrough the tyranny of racism in America was parallel to the ancient Israelis' struggle to break out of Egypt and to the Promised Land.

King was blessed by God to be a great orator and visionary. Many times during his life he would use the analogy of Moses leading his people out of the clutches of cruel Egyptian slave masters toward the Promised Land.

King was blessed by God to be a great orator and visionary. Many times during his life he would use the analogy of Moses leading his people out of the clutches of cruel Egyptian slave masters toward the Promised Land. He would use such imagery as he preached in churches and taught in synagogues. Indeed in an amazing American prophetic moment, on April 3, 1968, at Mason Temple in Memphis, Tennessee, Dr. King fervently spoke about being in the land of Israel as he gave what would be called his *"Mountain Top"* speech. During this famous American moment, Dr. King used his experience in the modern day country of Israel to better paint the New Testament story that Jesus told of the Good Samaritan. He spoke of traveling the road from Jerusalem to Jericho just as the Good Samaritan had traveled. He told of the winding mountain road that had numerous places for thieves to hide and why it was such a dangerous road to travel in Biblical times. By visiting Israel with his wife Coretta, he made a pilgrimage like so many millions of Christians have over the centuries and the powerful Holy Land of the Bible became like hues of color as Dr. King used words to paint a picture for the world to see. His picture was a picture of freedom and what it means to be truly free—free to be who God designed you to be.

Dr. King concluded his remarks, which were so sadly prophetic in one part by saying:

"Like anybody, I would like to live a long life. Longevity has its place. But I'm not concerned about that now. I just want to do God's will. And He's allowed me to go up to the mountain. And I've looked over. And I've seen the Promised Land. I may not get there with you. But I want you to know tonight, that we, as a people, will get to the Promised Land!"

Sadly, the next day Dr. King was assassinated. But what has been etched into the stone of history is the fact that just as blacks in America and all Americans together struggle on their journey to the Promised Land, so, too does the modern day country of Israel struggle against those foes who wish to push all the Jews into the sea. There is something about the Promised Land, the land flowing with milk and honey as testified in the Old Testament, that sets a goal, that gives destiny to a journey, and makes a struggle become a quest for freedom.

Dr. Martin Luther King, Jr.'s blessing to the nation of Israel was using the rich imagery of the land of the Bible and tying the destiny of any one or any group seeking freedom to the destiny of Israel being a free and prosperous country as the world's only Jewish state. As Dr. King used to preach that all men's destinies are tied together, we can grasp that the survival of Israel is tied to the destinies of all the nations on earth

The Fourth Blessing

A fourth American blessing in many ways has been forgotten, and it may be because of who provided the blessing, but without a doubt, this American blessed Israel in a special way. And it is worth noting that he was the only human on earth that could have provided this blessing at that time. In fact, as will be noted at the end of this chapter, it could not even be done today. This American blessing for Israel came during the October 1973 Yom Kippur War.

Henry Kissinger *(an American Jew, of German extraction)* had been named as President Nixon's new Secretary of State on September 22nd, just 14 days before the attack on Israel. Kissinger at first did not want to show an overabundance of support for Israel because he felt that might lead to an intensification of potential conflict with the USSR. Israel's Prime Minister Golda Meir and her defense team were not as successful militarily as the team of the Six Day War in 1967. But astonishing figures show that Egypt and Syria began the Yom Kippur conflict with 1,040 combat aircraft and lost 456 planes. The IAF *(Israeli Air Force)* lost 15 planes: 9 *(mostly American made A-4 Skyhawks)* to the Soviet made SA-6 missiles and another 6 in air-to-air combat. The loss ratio between the IAF and their adversaries was 18.4:1. Another internal American blessing came from two American Jewish IAF pilots who had flown F-4 Phantoms in the Vietnam War against Soviet missile defenses. These pilots taught their fellow IAF pilots how to defeat the SA-2 and SA-3 Soviet made missiles while flying F-4s and A-4s on strike and air superiority missions.

Much of the information about the Yom Kippur War has been provided by J. David Rogers. He is a former naval intelligence officer and a frequent contributor to the Proceedings. He is Professor and Hasselmann Chair in Geological and Petroleum Engineering at the Missouri University of Science and Technology. J. David Rogers says, "As Israel suffered a series of setbacks during the initial phases of the conflict, the Nixon Administration became increasingly concerned, seeing it as part of the continuing struggle between Soviet-backed aggressors and American-backed defenders *(like Korea and Vietnam)*.

As the situation between Israel and her Arab enemies seemed to stall, President Nixon requested authorization from Congress to send emergency aid to Israel, despite threats from the Persian Gulf members of OPEC that they would raise the price of crude oil by 70% in the wake of the conflict. This blatant retaliation served to entrench opposition to the emergency sales of arms to the Israelis, but Nixon held fast, ordering every available aircraft from the Military Airlift Command to be employed *(countermanding the recommended piecemeal shipments proposed by Kissinger)*, telling his aides *"We are going to get blamed just as much for three planes as for three hundred."* After several days of internal debates within his administration, Nixon's emergency airlift was code-named *"Operation Nickel Grass."*

President Nixon's bold leadership came through for the nation of Israel and this American blessing has been unequaled in its quickness and enormity. Rogers noted, *"567 supply missions were flown, delivering over 22,000 tons of supplies, with another 90,000 tons of bulk goods and ammunition stocks delivered to the Israelis by maritime sealift. Years later, former Israeli Prime Minister Golda Meir admitted that upon hearing of the massive American airlift during a meeting of her cabinet, she began to cry."*

Rogers mentioned that Americans did pay a price at the gas pump as OPEC initiated its first oil embargo. And as we mentioned in the opening paragraph, President Nixon's actions paved the way for the War Powers Resolution that Congress passed on November 7, 1973. This act limits any president's power to commit military assets to an armed conflict without the consent of Congress. Such a blessing by the decision by one person will not happen again.

Rogers also gave a personal note about this American President's blessing to the nation of Israel, *"For those of us who subsequently served as US CENTCOM intel officers, it's difficult to imagine how important this brave act on the part of Richard Nixon was, potentially saving Israel in their time of need. I doubt if we would come close to such action today."*

Four distinctly American blessings directly affecting the nation of Israel are truly treasures in the Land of the Bible. These four blessings came from four unique Americans, who loved their country, and also loved the people and the land of Israel. As God called forth these Americans the question must be asked, *"Is God calling you to be a blessing for the people and the land of Israel?"*

Dr. Edward Holliday is a sought-after speaker and author. His most recent book is entitled, *Bedrock Truths.*

CHAPTER SIX

Here am I, Lord, Send Me

Earl Cox

This was the response Isaiah gave when he heard God calling and, because of the lessons I've learned, it is the central theme for most of my speeches and the way I attempt to conduct my life.

I've known the Lord most all of my life, however He lived in my head and not in my heart and there's a vast difference. About 18 years ago is when I realized that "knowing about The Lord" is not at all the same as "knowing The Lord." This revelation and transformation took place in my life the day I heard The Lord calling me to become an advocate for Israel and the Jewish people. My faith in Jesus Christ moved from knowledge stored in my head to love embedded deep within my heart. The most important lesson I've learned along the way is that our Lord does not need any of us. All he desires is our obedience. God gives us opportunities followed by the freedom to choose. We may either accept or decline the opportunities he presents to us and He does not pick people for specific jobs based on education, qualifications or experience. In fact, it's generally the opposite. You see, the less qualified we are for the task He places before us, the more we must depend on Him versus relying on our own education, understanding and experience. Our Lord does, however, provide plenty of on-the-job training and He will always provide the necessary tools, however this is something I had to learn along the journey as I learned to trust Him more and to give Him first place in my life. It's not acceptable to bring Him our leftovers once we've self-indulged. Far too many try to pacify our Lord by giving Him our "spare" time or our "extra" resources but He expects the "first fruits." All that we have is a gift from Him to be used for His glory.

On that momentous day when The Lord called me to become an advocate for Israel, my initial instinct was to enroll in a school of theology. *"After all,"* I reasoned, *"how can I serve God without proper theological training?"* I prayerfully placed this before God and He answered almost immediately. The next morning The Lord took me to the passage in I John chapter 2 which says *"... ye need not that any man teach you..."* And so it has been with me ever since. The Lord gives me instructions one paragraph at a time and guides me one step at a time. By keeping me from knowing the *"big picture,"* He is keeping me from trying to get out in front and lead and so I must remain in prayer constantly seeking His direction.

So just how did God call me to become an outspoken advocate for Israel and the Jewish people? It was the result of my own personal *"Damascus Road"* experience. It was not something I created or crafted. At the time The Lord called me I was not even remotely interested in Israel and, as far as I knew, not involved or connected with any Jewish people. I had to study a map of the world to find tiny Israel's exact location. Truly God could not have picked a less qualified person in terms of worldly knowledge and experience as it relates to Israel and the Jews yet I knew it was The Lord calling. When, as a Christian, you know it's The Lord calling, what other response could there possibly be except, *"Yes, Lord, here am I."* It's important to insert a word of caution here. Far too many people become paralyzed by prayer. When you know it's The Lord speaking, what, exactly, is there to pray about? And so began my journey.

Armed with precious little knowledge about Israel and the Jewish people, I dove in heard first and almost drowned. I made assumptions that seemed logical but which were absolutely wrong. First of all, I believed that all

Christians were basically on the same theological page embracing Israel as God's special land and the Jews as His chosen people. Secondly, I believed that all Jewish people were, by nature, pro-Israel and, thirdly, I believed that Israelis and Jews would be thrilled to know that while they are being condemned by so many in the world, they have Christian friends who are emerging from the shadows to stand with them. Wrong, wrong and wrong again. Early on in my new walk with Israel during one of my initial visits to the Holy Land, God revealed to me that my *"Good News"* was not necessarily such good news for Israel and the Jews and He used a petit, middle-aged woman to bring me this enlightened message.

One afternoon following a meeting in the lobby of the Jerusalem Gold Hotel, I was introduced to a woman who was the daughter of Holocaust survivors. She relayed a chilling story to me that was like a giant spotlight illuminating a valuable truth that had been hidden from my eyes. The Christian legacy as it relates to the Jewish people is anything but good news. This is her mother's story. I pray it will help you mature in your understanding of Christian – Jewish relations just as it did for me.

Her story began from the cold barracks of a concentration camp on a wintry evening in December. The snow was a foot deep and the wind was blowing fiercely. Her mother's barrack, like all the others, was extremely cold with no heat, no insulation and with sizeable gaps between the boards of the wooden plank walls. The Jewish prisoners were dressed in threadbare clothing with rags wrapped around their feet in place of shoes. A few were lucky enough to have rough burlap sacks for blankets. All were hungry and many were starving. All were dirty, covered in lice and many were so ill as to be at death's door. As night fell, the field across the way became illuminated from the glow of the fireplace in the Nazi officers gathering hall. The darker the night grew, the brighter the glow that emanated from the warm fire inside the hall lighting up the field. Singing could be heard coming from inside. Peering through the gaps in the boards of the barracks, it was easy for the prisoners to see across the field and into the windows of the officers' mess where mugs of warm beverages were being enthusiastically consumed. The time of year on the Gregorian calendar marked it as Christmas and the song coming forth from the mouths of the savage Nazi tormentors was, *"Joy to the World."* For the Jews in that concentration camp who had already witnessed and experienced unspeakable horrors, there was absolutely no joy in the world. Sadly, this is how many Jewish people were introduced to Christians and the faith we embrace. How arrogant, or ignorant, I was to think that I would be welcomed as a friend by the people of Israel. Nothing I had ever been taught in church or Sunday school prepared me for the historical truth of why Jewish people have not been accepting of Christians but I felt compelled to learn more.

After having a chance to digest this story, I began to look at history – my Christian history – through a fresh set of eyes. I was surprised and appalled to learn that much of what Hitler did was in the name of Christianity and that his Nazi thugs and henchmen were not recruited from among the dregs of German society but rather were from the upper echelon, the educated, the elite. I was horrified to learn that some were even church leaders and pastors who, after the Holocaust, went back to pastoring churches ... Christian churches.

> **Holocaust education is carefully and meticulously taught to most all Jewish children but it is not taught so thoroughly in public or Christian schools and this is to our detriment.**

Holocaust education is carefully and meticulously taught to most all Jewish children but it is not taught so thoroughly in public or Christian schools and this is to our detriment. We've all heard the axiom that those who fail to learn history are doomed to repeat it. It's no secret that anti-Semitism is again on the rise around the world and even in the church - perhaps especially in the church. We failed our Jewish brothers and sisters during World War II as Hitler was rounding them up for extermination. Christian silence was deafening then just as it is now and many in the church are openly complicit through support for BDS campaigns which are blatant attacks against Israel and the Jewish people. How can we possibly claim to love Jesus and not also love His family? Words paved the way for the Holocaust during World War II and words are again paving the way for the rising tide of anti-Semitism in France and all of Europe, at the UN and, indeed, around the world. Each time the Jewish people commemorate the Holocaust and honor its victims they repeat the words, *"**Never Again!**"* These words must also become part of the Christian conversation. We must vow that never again will we turn a blind eye to the suffering of those who have been systematically marginalized and even demonized by society and its leaders and never again will we be silent in the face of discrimination and anti-Israel propaganda. But vowing is not enough. We must support our promise and stand by our convictions with actions. We cannot have one foot in the world and the other in the Kingdom. God does not embrace *"fence-straddlers."*

The next lesson I encountered hit me like a ton of bricks and it's called *"Replacement Theology."* This is a false teaching perpetrated within many mainstream Christian denominations which essentially states that God is through with the Jews, that the church has replaced Israel in God's sight and that Christians have replaced the Jews as God's chosen people. *"After all,"* many would reason, *"aren't the Jews responsible for the death of Jesus?"* Absolutely not! The Jews accused Him, the Romans executed Him but it was our sins which placed Him on that cross.

The third lesson I learned came from my mistaken assumption that all Jews naturally support Israel and her right to exist as a Jewish state. This is simply not the case. The Jews are s complicated people. While their differences are many, they also share much in common. Top of the list is the value Israelis place on life – all life and this include the lives of Palestinians. Next is the high value they place on family relationships and on friendships. So why don't all Jewish people support Israel? I've surmised that one possible reason is that many have taken up the cause of the underdog or those perceived as being the underdog, the marginalized or the oppressed wanting to protect others from the sufferings they have endured throughout history. It matters not that the underdog status portrayed by the Palestinians and others may be a fabrication of the liberal media and the expert Palestinian PR machine. Israelis are all too ready to accept the blame for problems. They've reached a point whereby they are ready to do just about anything for peace – even if it's only the promise of peace. Israelis are quick to stand up for the rights of others but not so quick to defend themselves. It's a paradox but it partly explains why many Jews are viewed as liberals. In stark contrast to the Palestinians, Israelis never accept the status of victimhood preferring instead to view themselves as thriving in spite of what they have suffered and endured throughout history. Even when confronted with evil, ugly acts of anti-Semitism and blatant injustice, it simply is not part of their culture to protest loudly in their own defense. This is what makes Christian support for Israel so important at this moment in time. We must stand up and speak out in support and defense of Israel and the Jewish people. If not us, then who? If not now, then when? Pray about it if you must, but don't be left behind. Our Lord's foot is surely on the threshold. He gives us a choice but doesn't wait indefinitely for us to accept. He will move on and give the task and the blessing that goes with it to another.

Building bridges of friendship and understanding between Christians and Jews requires a pure heart and clean hands.

History must not be allowed to repeat itself. Through our ancient faiths, Christians and Jews must form modern alliances. Building bridges of friendship and understanding between Christians and Jews requires a pure heart and clean hands. Those who attempt a back door approach in order to conceal a hidden agenda will not be successful. Our actions must speak louder than our words. Genuine love, openness, honesty and integrity are the pillars upon which any bridge linking Christians and Jews must be built. As Christians, we must be genuine through and through. What we do and say when people are watching is just as important as what we do and say when we think no one is watching. God will not be mocked. When touching the Jew, we are touching the *"apple of God's eye."* This is a phrase which refers to loving or cherishing something or someone above all others. No, Christians have not replaced the Jew and the Church has not replaced Israel. God is the same yesterday, today and forever. He is the Author and Giver of life and the Creator of the Universe. Christians owe the Jews a debt of gratitude. They were chosen by God to record, preserve and protect His Word and pass it down from generation to generation which they have faithfully accomplished. In the Book of Romans the Apostle Paul warns Christians not to be proud because it is not we who support the root, but the Root which supports us. Through Christ we Christians *(Gentiles)* have been grafted into the natural olive tree which, of course, means Israel. Through this grafting, God brought us in to a new relationship with Him. If we truly love Jesus, we must also love His family. An attack on the Jews is an attack on all who love God. We must live our lives being proactive and obedient servants of our Lord faithfully fulfilling the work He places before us even if it involves personal cost or sacrifice or does not fit conveniently with our personal plans.

We cannot dismiss The Lord and expect Him to bless us. Jesus will protect that which is His. After all, it's not what you know, it's Who you know!

Earl Cox is an international broadcaster and journalist who has served in senior level positions with four US presidents. Due to his outspoken support for Israel, he has been recognized by Prime Minister Netanyahu as a Good Will Ambassador from Israel to the Jewish and Christian communities around the world.

CHAPTER SEVEN

The Outlandish Charge of Israel as an Apartheid State

Malcolm Hedding

"Balak the king of Moab has brought me from Aram, from the mountains of the east. Come, curse Jacob for me, and come, denounce Israel! How shall I curse whom God has not cursed? And how shall I denounce whom the Lord has not denounced? For from the tops of the rocks I see him, and from the hills I behold him; there! A people dwelling alone, not reckoning itself among the nations." Numbers 23:7-9

Today it is both popular and politically correct to accuse Israel of being an apartheid state. This smear has been brought against the only democracy in the Middle East by the BDS movement (Boycott, sanction and divest from Israel) and by pro-Palestinian activists who have no interest in democratic government and real peace with Israel. The implications of this accusation are serious in that - if the original apartheid state, South Africa, had to be overthrown and dismantled as it was, then it stands to reason that the same must happen to Israel.

Of course this initiative to brand Israel a racist state is not new, as a similar attempt was made in 1975 at the United Nations when the General Assembly adopted a resolution defining Zionism as racism. After close scrutiny and investigation, this resolution was finally overturned in 1991 when it was established that in fact Zionism is nothing more than an ideology that gives expression to the longing of Jews everywhere to return to the land of their forefathers. However, not withstanding this setback, the enemies of Israel were determined to remodel the accusation and they did in the form of the current charge that Israel is an apartheid state.

So then the apartheid slur against the state of Israel is just another attempt to reintroduce the notion that Israel is a racist entity that must be dismantled in order to bring peace to the Middle East. Those who advocate for this position are invariably Islamists who wish to see Israel given over to the totalitarianism of radical Islam. That is, they would be more than happy to see Hamas or Hezbollah in control of the region! In fact at the very root of this new movement is the age-old problem of anti-Semitism.

I am a South African who was born in 1952 and was therefore raised in the apartheid state of South Africa. I saw the wickedness of this system firsthand; I lived in its world every day and witnessed the systematic dehumanization of 30 million black people by a white minority government. There is nothing in Israel that is even close to this abomination and to suggest that there is, is an insult to the millions of black people in South Africa who lived and suffered under it. The truth is, nowhere in Israel today are Arab Israelis treated in the manner in which the black people of South Africa were treated. Arab Israelis can go anywhere in the country, live anywhere they wish to, go to any university or educational institution or hospital of their choice and take up any profession they desire.

The apartheid state of South Africa, by contrast, passed laws that totally stripped the African people of having any stake in the land of their birth. These laws were draconian, inhumane and vicious and were the following:

- The Group Areas Act, that placed restrictions on where blacks could live.

- The Influx Control Act, that limited the movement of blacks in the country.

- The Job Reservation Act, which prohibited black people from taking up certain professions.

- The Bantu Education Act, which provided black children with an inferior education.

- The infamous Pass Laws Act, which temporarily legalized black people's presence in a certain region.

The latter meant that black people could not freely move around the country unless they were needed to provide labor for white owned industry etc. The "Pass" called a "Dom Pass" (Dumb Pass) by the black people legitimized their presence in a place that they would otherwise not be allowed to live in or operate in. The "Dom Pass" tightened up the restrictions outlined in the Influx Control Act. Black people were thus herded into "Locations" later called Townships, like Soweto, from where they served as cheap labor to the big "white by night" cities and industries. If caught out of their zone as designated by their Pass, they were immediately arrested and thrown into jail. Indeed, even if they were legitimately in the area but forgot to carry their Pass, they were still arrested and imprisoned. Their "Pass" governed their lives, designating their place of domicile, and had to be on them at all times.

In March 1960 anger and resentment in this regard boiled over and consequently some 5000 black people embarked on a peaceful protest at a police station in a place called Sharpeville. The response by the apartheid apparatus was swift and severe in that 69 people were gunned down and killed and a further 180 were wounded. According to the governing authorities, the blacks would be taught a lesson! Resistance would be met with "an iron fist" as one Nationalist Party leader put it.

According to the white minority government, Africans had inferior brains to whites and therefore they did not need or qualify for "white education." No, they were instead subjected to what was called Bantu Education, and to make matters worse, the Nationalist Afrikaner Government insisted that the language of education in black schools be that of Afrikaans! Black children could not be schooled in their mother tongue but in that of the oppressor. Consequently in 1976 the Soweto Riots broke out and swept through the whole country. The response of the government was swift and severe as once again thousands of blacks were indiscriminately shot and countless thousands more were arrested and put in jails.

Anti-apartheid activists like Steve Biko were murdered and others like Nelson Mandela were imprisoned on Robben Island just off the beautiful city of Cape Town. The Soweto Riots sparked the end of apartheid and from that time forward the only way the government could keep a lid on the resistance was to ring the African locations with what was called a "ring of steel." That is, tanks, armored cars and armed white soldiers surrounded the black townships. All this kept the white areas "black free" and in a false notion of peace. The country was boiling underneath as the vast black majority were totally disinvested and disenfranchised. The truth is, in apartheid South Africa black lives were cheap and expendable and many young desperate black people were hung for petty crimes like theft. Black lives did not matter!

The living conditions of black people were appalling to say the least as the sprawling black townships had little or no services. In the winter months a thick pall of grey smoke hung over these areas bringing with it all sorts of sickness and respiratory diseases. The misery of being born black in South Africa was indescribable and it was on the backs of their labor that the country was built and thrived. They were nothing more than cheap labor and they were routinely insulted and verbally abused by being called names, the worst of which was, "Kaffir"; a term borrowed by the nationalist government from the slave traders of Islam. Just as Islam punishes and abuses so called "infidels" so the South African government marginalized its black citizens and herded them into Gestapo like ghettos!

So then, to equate all of this with the nation state of Israel today is simply absurd and outrageous.

So then, to equate all of this with the nation state of Israel today is simply absurd and outrageous. Arab Israelis excel in all areas of Israel's economy; they have full representation in the Knesset (Parliament); they occupy positions on the High Court of Israel and officially represent Israel at international beauty and singing contests. There is precisely nothing that holds them back from achieving their dreams in the free and democratic state of Israel.

To be honest then, the real slur leveled at Israel as being an apartheid state is made against the nation in the context of its conflict with the Palestinians on the West Bank and in Gaza. In other words, this accusation is made within the framework of disputed territories only. However, those who make the accusation have sinister and wicked motives in that they really desire to use this accusation as one of the weapons they can wield in their desire to destroy all of Israel! They affirm this time and time again in the Arabic speaking media and the charters of Hamas and of the Palestinian Authority continue to call for the destruction of all of Israel thus also confirming this. They have no desire to come to a settled and peaceful accommodation with the State of Israel even though successive Israeli governments have endeavored to do so. The idea of two states living side by side in peace and security is not on their agenda and they say it all the time in Arabic. No, they wish to reclaim the lands once under the heel of Islam and this in turn means that the very existence of Israel is anathema to them.

To achieve this goal they wage a war of terror against Israel and they wage a diplomatic war against Israel in the halls of international institutions and on the college campuses of the West. The latter has taken the form of branding Israel an apartheid state. Those who use it and advance this narrative all over the world actually know nothing of apartheid and would not be able to properly define it if asked to. However, the word apartheid is a very emotive word and thus we can only oppose this lie with the truth. I know the truth because I grew up in apartheid South Africa and lived in the free democratic state of Israel for fourteen years. If one listens to the nightly broadcasts on TV of Hamas and the Palestinian Authority, one will quickly learn of their ultimate agenda, that of Israel's destruction. Sadly, Western politicians routinely laugh this off as mere rhetoric, just as they did some 70 years ago with Hitler's "rhetoric!"

The Oslo Accords of the 1990s nearly brought this unhappy episode to a conclusion, but at the very end of this initiative, Yasser Arafat withdrew, falsified reasons for doing so and began a war with Israel known as the Second Intifada. His wife Suha Arafat later confirmed that he did so because he was not prepared to give the "Islamic Heritage" as she put it, of his people to the Jews, meaning that he could not adhere to the peace accords he had agreed to as these only gave the Palestinians a portion of the land and not all of Israel. In fact after the Presidential Inauguration of Nelson Mandela in April 1994, Arafat, speaking in a Mosque in Johannesburg, confirmed that his peace agreement with Israel, signed on the lawns of the White House with Prime Minister Rabin and President Clinton in 1993, was nothing more than a deception designed to buy time in order to pursue the greater goal of Israel's total destruction.

No my friends, Israel is not an apartheid state in any shape or form. Her restrictions on Palestinians in the disputed territories are designed for only one purpose, and this includes the security wall, to stop Palestinian terror squads from assaulting her towns and villages. In this regard they have been successful and any democracy under sustained assault would do the same. In fact, Israel is a bright light in the Middle East of civilized democratic governments and recently Arab journalists in Egypt and elsewhere in the region have acknowledged this. For sure even the so-called moderate Arab nations in the region, like Saudi Arabia and Jordan, remain dictatorships with restrictions and laws that sometimes shadow the apartheid state! Women live under severe restrictions, their testimony in a court of law is not equal to that of a man, they are banned from driving cars and barred from certain professions. Add to this the fact that the press is not truly free and must tow the government line and the fact that people of other faiths cannot practice their religion freely and that Muslims who convert to another religion are executed publicly then the picture you have is of another version of apartheid! Who can deny it?

South Africa underwent a remarkable change in that the apartheid government realized that it could not continue to rule the black majority in a manner that robbed them of their human dignity. It therefore decided to genuinely sue for peace and this required the very bold step of surrendering power to a black majority democratic government. President F. W. de Klerk found a genuine peace partner in Nelson Mandela and together they forged a new day for all of South Africa's people. The only apartheid state collapsed and, as they say, the rest is history. Sadly, Israel has yet to find a genuine peace partner who does not have her total destruction in mind. Until such a person comes forward, she will have to be vigilant and watchful while at the same time continuing to strengthen her democratic institutions, which are indeed the envy of the world.

Golda Meir, the Prime Minister of Israel, once said, " Until the Palestinians love their children more than they hate the Jews there will be no peace in the region." She was right and sadly it seems that more lives will be lost as long as the Palestinians and their sponsors from Iran and elsewhere continue to wage war against Israel. They will fail, as will the BDS movement and the Israel Apartheid movement, because the truth will always overcome the darkness of lies and deceit. Mahmoud Abbas, the Palestinian Authority President, is an example of this type of wickedness because he continues to assert, in the light of overwhelming evidence to the contrary, that the Holocaust never happened. It is impossible to negotiate with a man like this who is intellectually dishonest and incapable of telling the truth at anytime. It is no wonder that he and his fellow terrorists continue to peddle the lie that Israel is an apartheid state.

Malcom Hedding served for 10 years as Executive Director of the International Christian Embassy Jerusalem. He is the author of numerous books including *The Basis of Christian Support for Israel.*

CHAPTER EIGHT

The Threat of Militant Islam

Bruce Assaf

In order to understand militant Islam you have to understand the prophet Muhammed. With over a billion followers and growing, he is the model for all human conduct. To the Muslim he is the embodiment of the will of God (Allah). Muhammed's behavior is an example to all Muslims and cannot be criticized. It is difficult to grasp the meaning of Islam's continuing conflict and radical ideology unless you know the man who initiated that conflict.

Unlike Jesus, the man Muhammed was both a spiritual and political figure, a religious prophet and a military conqueror. As Muslims believe Muhammed taught absolute truth, it is therefore God's will (Allah) for them to rule the earth. This combination has led his followers, both ancient and contemporary, to the belief that an Islamic theocracy is where the world is heading. This means that in time, all the peoples of the world will ultimately accept the Prophet and his version of Allah. The thrust behind militant Islam.

The life of Muhammed can be divided into two parts, the tolerant years in Mecca and the aggressive years in Medina. When Muhammed began to preach his revelations from Allah, as he claimed, he believed a peaceful religion was a good strategy for attracting others to the teachings of Islam, especially the Jewish people. When his attempts to win over the Jews through peaceful coexistence were not successful, a new strategy was launched based on power. This is when he declared jihad (holy war). He went out to convert nonbelievers to Islam by the sword.

Modern Muslims contend that the term jihad pertains only to the inner struggle of the human soul against temptation and spiritual evil. They sugar-coat the clear record in history. Militant Islamic groups throughout the world shout "Jihad, jihad, for the sake of Allah". It is not in any way to exhort their troops and individual followers to wage a battle for the soul. There is a blessing for those who fight jihad, according to the Qur'an:
"Then verily, thy Lord, will be forgiving and merciful for those who left their homes after they had been tried and then carried out Jihad and were steadfast" (Surah 16:110).

According to the Qur'an, true Muslims are those who carry out jihad. The Qur'an states, "Those who believe and have fled and fought strenuously in Allah's cause, and those who have given a refuge and a help, those it is who believe; to them is forgiveness and generous provision due" (Surah 8:74). Forgiveness and provision will be given to those who fight or provide help and asylum for jihadists. Islamic tradition tells us how he fought in battles, and how he had enemies murdered and had prisoners executed. Militancy is inbreed within Islam. Muhammed taught:

"The punishment of those who wage war against Allah and His Messenger, and strive with might and main for mischief through the land is: execution, or crucifixion, or the cutting off of hands and feet from opposite sides, or exile from the land: that is their disgrace in this world, and a heavy punishment is theirs in the Hereafter" (Surah 5:33).

Armed with their apostle's battle cry, the forces of Islam began a reign of terror unparalleled in history. Their first target was the Arabian Peninsula. In a series of brutal military actions the forces of Islam killed, captured, or forced the conversion of virtually every inhabitant of the Arabian Peninsula. From that moment on, this part of the world was subjected to Islam and later to what is called Sharia Law.

During the next 100 year period, the forces of Islam conquered all of North Africa, Palestine/the Holy Land, Turkey, Asia Minor, Spain and parts of France until they were stopped by Charles Martel at the battle of Tours in 732. It has been shown recently that the native populations of England, Germany Italy, Scandinavian countries, and France are shrinking, while the immigrant population of Muslims in these countries is expanding. France is home to over 5.5 million Muslims, the largest population of Muslims in Western Europe. The Islamic world counts for a fifth of mankind.

Islam follows a theology of triumphalism. It is "the dominance of one's nation, ideology, or religious creed over another." Peace to a follower of Islam is when the the Jews are wiped off the map and no longer occupy the land of Israel. While Israel's enemies and those well-intentioned allies call for incremental steps for peace, they are in fact incremental steps for Israel's demise.

Militant Islam presents a more dangerous threat because it is not a nation, but a radical ideology that crosses borders, governments, territories and time lines without restraint. There is no single army, no commander and no central government in control. North African immigrants to Western Europe who would have once called themselves Tunisian, Iraqi or Turkish today, in growing numbers, consider their primary identity to be Muslim.

Our generation is seeing this fundamentalism infiltrate and take over entire nations. Like Iran, once a modern and prosperous country is now ruled by an oppressive regime that has become a platform for worldwide terrorism supporting the insurgencies of Hamas, Hezbollah and al-Quaeda. We have seen that same threat influence the policy and politics of western nations like France. Experts project by the year 2040, 80 percent of France will be Muslim.

Terrorism is only a single tactic. The true threat to Judeo-Christianity is the explosive growth of the radical Islamic theology. Not only are we being attacked from outside our borders, we are being infiltrated from within. The blows Israel has received since its re-establishment in 1948, and the intense hatred to destroy the Jewish nation, is what America and the world now face with greater threat.

Muslims see Israel as a thorn in their side. Many are taught that Abraham was a Muslim and the Jews have no right to the Temple Mount, or the land. The Jews are infidels who have stolen the promises and must be removed from the land. Jews and Christians having their presence in the city where the third holiest mosque of Islam sits is blasphemy to a Muslim. The re-establishment of Israel as a nation has brought both fear and anger to Muslims. The religious beliefs of Judaism and Islam are in total opposition to each other. In the eyes of Islam the Jews are the occupation and must be evicted from the land.

Islam is more than a mere religion. In essence Islam is a political system and ideology within a religious framework.

Islam is more than a mere religion. In essence Islam is a political system and ideology within a religious framework. It is a system that lays down detailed rules for society and the life of every person. Islam means "submission" and it wants to dictate every aspect of life and is not compatible with freedom and democracy because of what it strives for is sharia law. In comparison to anything, it can be compared to Communism or national-socialism which are all totalitarian ideologies.

Winston Churchill called Islam"the most retrograde force in the world," and is why he compared Mein Kamph to the Qur'an. And with the Palestinian narrative as seeing Israel as the occupation and aggressor, the Israeli-Palestinian conflict is in reality a war against all things Jewish, modern and Western. It is a war between the God of the Bible and the god of the Qur'an, and not necessarily between Arab and Jew. The very roots are more than political; they are in fact spiritual, thus the term "holy war."

In 1947, when the UN voted to create a Jewish state, Haj Amin al-Husseini, the grand mufti of Jerusalem declared, "The entire Jewish population must be destroyed or driven into the sea. Allah has bestowed us the rare privilege of finishing what Hitler only began. Let the jihad begin; murder the Jews, murder the Jews, murder all of them."

Islam's agenda is both practical and prophetic. The practical plan is to expand the Islamic crescent from its Middle East stronghold into Europe and Asia, and eventually dominate the large cities in North America. Their prophetic agenda is to ensure that predictions and traditions of its founder, Muhammed, are fulfilled. And despite hearing the smooth tongue of well-educated Muslims telling the West there is no need for concern, the sword of militant Islam is slashing its way through the nations just as in Muhammed's day.

Today, radical Islam grows under the guise of tolerant compromise. To deny this, and the reality of Islam's determined goal for dominance throughout the world, is a dangerous refusal and denial that will continue to see America and the world experience continuing severe consequences from this ideology. Israel is all too familiar with militant Islam's determined goal to exterminate her. It is a holy war against all Jews just as Muhammed himself declared: "The last hour will not come until the Muslims fight the Jews, and the Muslims kill them." As Israel's enemies have repeatedly attacked the Jewish state, their determined goal is complete annihilation of Israel. Their dream is to destroy Israel. Israel now is simply receiving the blows that are meant for Western culture. It is a fight to undermine and destroy Western culture; to replace the Judeo-Christian foundations and culture and subjugate the world to the law of Islam.

Militant Islamic fundamentalists' war against the Jews and the West is seen by the media and the world as terrorism. It is terrorism, but more than that, the fact is that Muslims are simply being true to Islam. The Qur'an declares: *"Take not the Jews and Christians as friends. Slay the idolaters wherever you find them. Besiege them and prepare for them each ambush"* (Surah 9:5).

Extermination of Israel is bred into Muslims. After Muhammed ascended to power in Medina, he attempted to convert the Jews, from whom he had learned much. Muhammed initially instructed Muslims to bow toward Jerusalem when they prayed and observe the Jewish Day of Atonement. He also included Jewish patriarchs in the lore of Islam. Muhammed's knowledge of Judaic scripture, when compared to the learning of local Jewish scholars, was so flawed that the Jews ridiculed him, rejecting his claim to be God's greatest Prophet. When Jewish scholars remained true to their ancient faith the Prophet turned on them in anger. As a result, in the Qur'an, Allah, as quoted by Muhammed saying:

"Because of their iniquity, we forbade the good things which were formerly allowed them; because time after time they have debarred others from the path of Allah ; because they practice usury - though they were forbidden it- and cheat others of their possessions" (4:16).

The Qur'an further attacks Jews by calling them blasphemers and corrupters, a people unworthy of their heritage:

"Those to whom the burden of the Torah was entrusted and yet refused to bear it are like a donkey laden with books" (62:5).

The beginnings of Islam as taught and introduced by Muhammed's foundational teachings are the very root of militant Islam.

The beginnings of Islam as taught and introduced by Muhammed's foundational teachings are the very root of militant Islam. If Israel is to survive, then Islamic theology is not true. If Islam does not defeat Israel and remove the Jewish nation, Muhammed and the Qur'an were wrong. To a Muslim, that is absolutely unthinkable.

The religion of Islam, as compared to Judaism is this: Judaism is based on the unique historical event of a divine revelation experienced by an entire nation. Islam, however, is based on the prophetic claims of a single individual who subsequently convinced others to follow his ways.

Muhammad, slaughtered thousands of people in establishing and spreading Islam. He told his followers, "Who relinquishes his faith, kill him. I have been ordered by Allah to fight with people till they testify there is no god but Allah, and Muhammed is his messenger." The followers of militant Islam see these doctrines express the belief that Allah has commanded them to conquer the nations of the world both by cultural invasion and by the sword. And, according to the Qur'an, true Muslims are those who carry out jihad. We read from the Qur'an, *"Those who believe and have fled and fought strenuously in Allah's cause, and those who have given a refuge and a help, those it is who believe; to them is forgiveness and generous provision due" (Surah 8:74).*

The entire Middle East is inflamed by this bloodthirsty rhetoric. And much of it with the echo of Muhammed's seventh-century call to drive Christians and Jews from the Arabian Peninsula and beyond. And, as it was then, so it is now with militant Islam. Radical Islamic fundamentalists believe that they have the anointed right to declare war on all those who resist Allah and his messenger Muhammed. The militants and radicals refer to Israel as "little Satan," and the United States as "big Satan." Militant Islam has its particular practice and interpretation of a very particular set of religious, political and social principles, which fuels the religious hatred that makes it so deadly to the enemies of Islam, namely the infidels. *"Give not way to the infidels, but by means of this Qur'an strive against them with a mighty strife" (Surah 25:54).*

The beliefs of Islam will not be totally realized nor the teachings of Muhammed fulfilled until Israel is defeated and exterminated. Islamic theology declares this, and in doing so it will be Allah's will for them to take back Jerusalem for their capital and the country of Israel for their possession and to again rule the earth to ensure that the predictions and teachings of its prophet, Muhammed.

And now, for the first time in 200 years, a violent strain of Islam is on the march, swarming across the Middle East like locusts, occupying vast amounts of land, terrorizing and executing the infidels. They have rallied and radicalized Muslims to form a world-wide Caliphate. In many parts of the world murder is justified if you are a non-believer. With a seventh-century medieval ideology, they are armed with 21th century weapons and technology employing numerous ground attacks. They believe such a military campaign on the ground would mobilize millions of Muslims into the final worldwide confrontation --- the long predicted ultimate holy war.

With 1.75 billion Muslim adherents, 10 per cent or more are militant extremists, This counts for millions of radical Muslims acting in the name of deity, motivated to impose a barbaric religion. The spirit of Haman and the spirit of Hitler is alive and active mobilizing with force and determination to wipe out Israel and the West. The resurgence of a militant Islam now threatens the stability of most of the governments in the Middle East.

Iran is racing to acquire nuclear weapons. It is radical Islam's and Iran's intention to destabilize not only the Middle East but the world. Fundamental

Islamic ideology is under the influence of the Islamic Revolutionary Government of Iran. Its goal of nuclear power is what is giving rise to an outright war for Islamic world domination. As America has lifted sanctions under the Obama administration, it is paving the way for a nuclear holocaust.

The rise of Islam, and in particular radical Islamic terrorism, strikingly foreshadows Ezekiel's great prophecy of (38 and 39). If politicians are reluctant, it is imperative for the church to lead the way in bringing the needed understanding of the times in this critical and crucial hour of history. (1 Chronicles 12:32)

Bruce Assaf is the founder of Blow the Trumpet International. He is the author of numerous books including *Charting Your Course to Win God's Way* and *Behind the Veil of Radical Islam: The Coming War*.

CHAPTER NINE

White House Policy and the Effect on Israel from Statehood to the Present

William Koenig

There are five great items of evidence that exist today and which nobody can deny or fail to recognize which support the trustworthiness of the Bible. The first is the Jews.[1] —Robert Dick Wilson

In the anxious moments and days that fell in the shadow of the death of Franklin Delano Roosevelt—on vacation at his Warm Springs, Georgia, retreat—the West's political and military leadership breathed a sigh of relief that the twilight of the Axis Powers had come ... at the same time a hapless politician from Missouri took the driver's seat in the Oval Office. Harry S. Truman didn't have the education, social background, breeding, or apparent leadership qualities to maneuver America through a new time of challenge

---

1 Robert Dick Wilson, The Princeton Theological Review, "The Rule of Faith and Life," 430, July 1928.

as the Soviet Union took advantage of a war-weary Europe to gobble up territory for its evil empire.

Truman was so much dull dishwater in the wake of the charismatic Roosevelt's sudden death, barely a few months into his fourth term. The iconic decisions about Japan were still months away. And then something amazing happened. Harry Truman emerged as a fearless, visionary leader. His successful prosecution of the last months of the war tagged him at least as a man who would not roll over. He would need all that grit, for a truly epic decision lay before him only three years after the war ended. In late 1947, yet another epic decision lay before Truman.

Palestine.

As the Zionist leaders in the region and in Europe understood, it was now or never after UN Resolution 181 paved the way for a Jewish (and Palestinian Arab) state in historical Palestine. Jewish influencers began to jockey for meetings with Truman and his advisors, but they were rebuffed initially, for various reasons.

David Ben Gurion knew that his team must seize the day as the countdown for Britain's pullout of Palestine began. The empire set a date of May 15, 1948, to leave the area to the battling Jews and Arabs. As the burgeoning Jewish state needed the backing of a certain superpower, Truman found himself a popular man. He also found himself on the cusp of a pivotal moment in history, when his background would prepare him for the task at hand.

Truman's thinking on the Middle East was colored by his Baptist upbringing. Thoroughly versed in Scripture and its depictions of sacred landscapes, Truman, much like American presidents of an earlier time, possessed a detailed knowledge of Middle Eastern geography. "It wasn't just the Biblical part of Palestine that interested me," he recalled. "The whole history of that area of the world is just about the most complicated and most interesting of any anywhere." That fascination was on display in the Oval Office, where the president stunned General Eisenhower and Undersecretary of State Dean Acheson, both of whom thought him ignorant of the subject, by lecturing them on the strategic importance of the Middle East while referring to his personal, dog-eared map.[2]

So it was that when Ben Gurion and Co. gathered to announce the establishment of the new Jewish state (no one knew what it would even be called), they tensely monitored any possible decision by Truman and the United States to formally recognize them. As it was, of Truman's circle of advisors, only White House counsel Clark Clifford thought the president should recognize the fledgling state. Secretary of State George Marshall threatened to campaign against Truman during that election year if he chose to side with the Zionists.

Finally, Israel's first cabinet met at 4:00 p.m. on the afternoon of May 14, in a nondescript building near the beach at Tel Aviv. Ben Gurion rose to read from a document (written in Hebrew!). Hours later, Truman sent a spokesman into a hallway to read a brief statement to the press:

"This Government has been informed that a Jewish state has been proclaimed in Palestine, and recognition has been requested by the Provisional government thereof.

The United States recognizes the Provisional government as the de facto authority of the new State of Israel. With his own hand, the president had written "State of Israel."

Thus began a relationship between American presidents and Israel that stood many a test. Until Barack Hussein Obama.

From the corridors of history, we hear the exchanges between Truman and Ben Gurion, Johnson and Eshkol, even Nixon and Meir. While each was a unique and complex relationship, mutual respect reigned. Even Richard Nixon, who was known to throw out an anti-Semitic remark or two, ordered his joint chiefs to *"send everything that will fly"* to rearm embattled Israel during the 1973 Yom Kippur War.

In the summer of 2014, Barack Obama ordered a halt to munitions sent to Israel to answer the deadly rocket fire of Hamas, from the Gaza Strip.

---

2   Oren, Power, Faith, and Fantasy, 476.

On April 18, 2016, a homicide bomber detonated himself onboard an Israeli bus in Jerusalem. The ensuing fireball injured twenty people. One mother spoke of looking up through the haze of smoke in the aftermath and seeing her burned daughter nearby. Though the Israelis are very good at responding to security threats—it was the first such bus bombing in years—it reinforced the point that terrorists like Hamas are still active, dedicated to fulfilling their charter of wiping out the Jewish state. The next day, U.S. Vice President Joe Biden, speaking at a left-wing gathering for J Street in Washington, made an incredible statement; he claimed that the administration experienced "overwhelming frustration"[3] with ... Israeli Premier Benjamin Netanyahu! As has become common practice among Western political elites, Biden unwittingly fulfilled Biblical prophecy by calling good evil and evil good (Isaiah 5:20). For decades, but accelerating since the doomed Oslo Accords in 1993, Western diplomats and politicians have never missed an opportunity to bash Israel, while giving a pass to the murderous PLO/Palestinian Authority, which has radicalized Palestinian society for a quarter century, much of it at the expense of the American taxpayer.

The entire Barack Obama presidency was spent undermining Israel consistently. As has been discussed, we don't have to look very far to understand why Obama has the worldview he has. Just ahead of the Jerusalem terror attack, Obama's former pastor, Jeremiah Wright, blasted Israel and called Jesus a "Palestinian." America's official turn away from Israel is but one sign that the United States, the world's greatest experiment in democracy, will not survive the Marxist/Socialist underpinnings of Obama's successful attempt to fundamentally transform the country. How did we get here?

Friends for Life

Except for a few rough waters with the Eisenhower Administration and again under Jimmy Carter, Israel has enjoyed a remarkably flourishing relationship with the United States from the beginning.

Few know that John F. Kennedy (and brother Bobby a decade later) visited Israel—or Palestine, as it was then known—in 1939. His impressions, all the more remarkable given the fact that his father Joe Kennedy was a notorious

---

3 http://www.cnn.com/2016/04/19/politics/biden-netanyahu-frustration-israel-j-street/

anti-Semite, are amazing. Kennedy, then a young man of twenty-one, was a keen observer of human nature, and this greatly aided him decades later in the White House. During his time in Palestine, he formed views that would provide the basic foundation of US foreign policy in the region for decades. Writing to his father in 1939, he advocated pragmatism: I see no hope for the working out of the British policy as laid down in the White Paper. As I said above, theoretically it sounds just and fair, but the important thing and the necessary thing is not a solution just and fair but a solution that will work.

Apart from this, Kennedy admired the Zionist work ethic, and his warm relationship with David Ben Gurion a generation later would help the still-growing Jewish state move into modernity.

Of course, Kennedy's successor would prove to be a valuable friend as well. Lyndon Johnson advised the Israelis to stand down in the wake of Nasser's bellicosity in the spring of 1967, but there is no reason to believe he would not have intervened militarily had the Israelis needed it—even though his administration was already bogged down in Vietnam.

Publicly, Johnson wished to be seen as even-handed:

The President indicated to [Israeli Ambassador Abba] Eban that before the United States took any forceful action, he would have to get a resolution from Congress. To Eban, this was waffling badly. For that would probably take weeks of bitter debate.[4]

We discussed Richard Nixon's positive response to Golda Meir's pleas a few years later, and we then move into the somewhat difficult Jimmy Carter years.

The one-term president seemed to genuinely dislike Menachem Begin and virtually forced the Israelis to Camp David. Still, it must be remembered that the *"cold peace"* the trio of Carter/Begin/Sadat forged in 1979 has lasted to this day.

Carter's bizarre meddling—and apparent anti-Semitism—emerged years later. In his 2006 book, Palestine: Peace, Not Apartheid, the former president used incendiary language even in the book's title (*Israel is in no way, shape, or* form an *"apartheid"* state, with Arabs holding positions of power in government, etc.). He also filled his book with outright falsehoods:

Palestine: Peace, Not Apartheid, Page 50: 'Perhaps the most serious omission of the Camp David talks was the failure to clarify in writing Begin's verbal promise concerning the settlement freeze during subsequent peace talks.'

Fact: Menachem Begin promised in the Camp David discussions to maintain a three-month settlement freeze and he adhered to his commitment. This was dramatically underscored in a public forum about the Camp David agreements on September 17, 2003 at the Woodrow Wilson Center. A member of the panel, Israeli jurist Aharon Barak, explained he had attended the relevant meeting at which the settlement freeze discussion transpired, had been the only one present taking notes, and that his notes showed Begin had agreed only to a three month freeze.

Ronald Reagan of course was a great friend to Israel, even though the Israeli airstrike on Iraq's Osirak nuclear reactor *(which saved Allied forces a decade later!)* was carried out without informing the president ahead of time.

Cracks began to appear, however, beginning with George Herbert Walker Bush *(my book, Eye to Eye: Facing the Consequences of Dividing Israel, chronicles the pitfalls faced by America whenever she stood against the Jewish state)*. It was Bush 41 who threatened to withhold loans to Israel, unless Yitzhak Shamir would sit at the negotiating table with the PLO.

This led to the famous Oslo Accords, the *"land-for-peace"* concept that has proven to be a dismal failure in light of constant Palestinian refusal to live in peace with the Jews.

The Bill Clinton years saw more consistent diplomatic effort, as the president worked hard for an Israeli-Palestinian Accord, to cement his legacy.

George W. Bush appeared to be a great friend of the Israelis, particularly Prime Minister Ariel Sharon, and he bound the United States to certain security guarantees, if they would divide the land and make painful concessions.

In November 2007, President Bush invited Israeli Prime Minister Ehud Olmert and Palestinian leader Mahmoud Abbas to Washington for the Annapolis Conference. There, he said,

"Achieving this goal requires neighbors committed to peace between Israel and a new Palestinian state—and I'm encouraged by the presence of so many here."

As usual, when it got down to brass tacks, it was Israel that was expected to make concessions, further shrinking an already dangerously small country.

Notice I didn't say that some of the participants in this flawed peace process were insincere.

This effort on the part of American presidents, beginning with Carter, to intervene personally to put an end to hostilities, was still done in a climate of genuine friendship between the two countries. Even Carter's alleged anti-Semitism didn't unravel the unique relationship between the countries.

All that changed in January 2009.

Barack Hussein Obama Assumes the Presidency

A totally new kind of American president strode onto the stage of history when the former constitutional law professor came to Washington.

Within weeks he sent serious positive signals to the Muslim Brotherhood in Cairo, Obama described this country's friendship with Israel as *"unbreakable."*

For myriad reasons—not the least of which is the newly inked agreement with Iran, which places Israel in existential danger—Obama has worked tirelessly to disrupt the friendship.

It seems to have begun with his bungling *(managing?)* of the so-called Arab Spring, when fighting between jihadists and regime loyalists in North African countries led the Middle East into a cauldron of terrorism, death, and destruction.

Unbreakable?

From the moment he entered office, Obama has fed a serious personal dislike of Benjamin Netanyahu.

For most, the contrast in every way between the two men could not be more stark.

Netanyahu, raised on a Zionist ethic by his father, Benzion *(himself a key member of the team that created the conditions for statehood)*, served in Israel's elite counter-terrorism unit, Sayeret Matkal. When his older brother, Jonathan, was killed leading the famous raid at Entebbe in 1976 *(perhaps the most successful hostage-rescue of all time)*, Benjamin changed the focus of his career from business to politics. He has said many times that Entebbe altered the trajectory of his life.

Israel has benefitted from this.

At the same time, Obama heaped around himself radical Marxist professors, friends, and advisors. His sympathy for the Palestinian cause *(read: the liquidation of Israel)* began in earnest in Chicago. His deeply anti-Semitic pastor, the Rev. Jeremiah Wright of Trinity United Church of Christ, educated him on Liberation Theology, the joint story of oppression crafted by '60s radicals in the United States and Palestinian journalists and religious figures even today.

Obama's loathing of Israel also explains how he can obscenely criticize Netanyahu and our ally Israel, while at the same time claiming he couldn't *"meddle"* in the corrupt Iranian elections of 2009, when the mullahs in Tehran were teetering on the edge of collapse.

Prop up Iran, tear down Israel.

It is important to note, too, that Obama hasn't even a shred of biblical worldview. In fairness, the same thing can be said for scores of American diplomats and politicians, who have forced on Israel the disastrous land-for-peace formula. The president and Beltway insiders have probably never heard of Joel 3:2:

I will also gather all nations, and will bring them down into the valley of Jehoshaphat, and will plead with them there for my people and for my heritage Israel, whom they have scattered among the nations, and parted my land.

Obama would no doubt laugh at the concept of divine retribution for breaking his commands, but the fact is, Western powers have set themselves up for divine judgment, based on *"land-for-peace."*

Consider the very small following sampling of anti-Israel measures and anti-Jewish though brought about by Obama:

A reduction in the sale of "bunker-buster" bombs, which would greatly aid an Israeli airstrike on Iran's nuclear facilities.

In April 2009, mere weeks after Obama assumed office, the United States allowed Turkey to provide weapons and training for the Lebanese Army, which had threatened Israel.

(In a remarkably bipartisan show of support to Israel, by contrast, Rep. Steny Hoyer visited Israel in 2009 and pointed out in a press conference that 368 out of 435 members of the House of Representatives had sent Obama a letter supporting Israel in its right to defend itself.)

In August 2009, Obama addressed one thousand rabbis in Washington, attempting to gain support for his radical healthcare overhaul. As Jews pray that they will be included in the Book of Life, Obama referred to those prayers and said: *"We are God's partners in matters of life and death."*

Except that no observant Jew would believe that. One writer at the time, Andrew Klavan, noted Jeremiah 1:5 and Job 38:17, in which the Lord's power and wisdom are seen as infinitely greater than mortal man, whom he would not *"consult"* for anything.

Obama blithely ignores such *"blunders,"* further exposing his anti-Jewish bias.

It is with regard to Obama's dangerously matter-of-fact *"deal"* with Iran that one can see his callous disregard for Israel.

The Apple of God's Eye

Barack Obama masked his hatred for Israel while campaigning for the presidency. Actually, the lies he told as a candidate (*"We will always support Israel's right to defend itself"*) are stock-in-trade for most politicians. During the 2016 presidential primary race, several Republican candidates pledged to move the American embassy from Tel Aviv to Jerusalem to fulfill a law passed by Congress in 1995. In fact, every American president since Oslo has utilized a little-known clause that allows him to indefinitely delay the moving of the embassy—ostensibly this is done not to offend the Palestinians and prejudice so-called *"final status"* issues. Never mind the Palestinians have done virtually nothing in twenty-five years to forge a real peace.

It is almost impossible in today's political climate to find a politician who really understands the implications of a reborn nation of Israel. If you look at a guidebook of members of Congress, you'll see that when it comes to religious affiliation, most are of a mainline or Catholic Church background.

In other words, they know nothing about Bible prophecy and don't care to know. This directly impacts how they attempt to force peace between Israel and the Palestinians. And it doesn't matter who is president, or who his secretary of state is. Warren Christopher saw the Arab-Israeli conflict the same way Colin Powell saw it: in purely secular terms.

There is and has been a disconnect between Washington, London, Paris, etc., and the truths of the Bible. Interestingly, in American history, several presidents have understood the specialness of the Jewish people, but today we are far removed from the character-driven presidencies of men like John Adams.

Obama's Undermining of Israel

From his choreographed speech in Cairo in 2009, Barack Obama has signaled to the world's most radical Muslim terrorists that he intended to cut Israel loose. In modern diplomatic parlance, this was called *"putting daylight"* between the two long allies. Israeli diplomats like Israeli Ambassador Michael Oren sounded this exact alarm and were roundly denounced by establishment-types in Washington.

In the spring of 2016, only days after Benjamin Netanyahu declared that the strategic Golan Heights would forever remain part of Israel, the Obama Administration said the exact opposite:

TEL AVIV—The Obama administration does not consider the Golan Heights part of Israel, U.S. State Department spokesperson John Kirby stressed Monday night, a day after Prime Minister Benjamin Netanyahu vowed that the Golan *"will forever remain under Israeli sovereignty"*.

"The U.S. position on the issue is unchanged," Kirby told reporters during a daily briefing at the State Department in Washington. ***"This position was maintained by both Democratic and Republican administrations. Those territories are not part of Israel and the status of those territories should be determined through negotiations. The current situation in Syria does not allow this,"*** Kirby continued.

On Sunday [April 17], Netanyahu opened a meeting with the Israeli cabinet on the issue of the Golan with the declaration that *"the Golan Heights will always remain under Israeli control."*[4]

No previous American president has had so strained a relationship with Israel as Barack Obama.

Lest one think these assertions are the product of a Bible-thumper, consider the following:

No previous American president has had so strained a relationship with Israel as Barack Obama. As Israeli Ambassador Michael Oren said in 2010,

"Israel's ties with the United States are in their worst crisis since 1975 ... a crisis of historic proportions." Author and scholar Dennis Prager concurred, "Most observers, right or left, pro-Israel or anti-Israel, would agree that Israeli-American relations are the worst they have been in memory."

In the spring of 2011, David Parsons, spokesman for the International Christian Embassy Jerusalem, said: *"There's a traditional, special relationship between America and Israel that Obama is basically throwing out the*

---

4 http://www.breitbart.com/jerusalem/2016/04/19/obama-administration-golan-heights-not-part-israel/

window in a sense." David Rubin, a U.S.-born Israeli author and expert on the Middle East, put it this way:

"President Obama is very harmful for Israel and very dangerous for the future of Judeo-Christian civilization."

The author and economist Thomas Sowell asserted that Obama's relationship with Israel had been consistent with the president's pattern of *"selling out our allies to curry favor with our adversaries."* Political analyst Charles Krauthammer observed that Obama had *"undermined"* Israel as a result of either his *"genuine antipathy"* toward the Jewish state or *"the arrogance of a blundering amateur."* In October 2012, Israeli lawmaker Danny Danon, chairman of Likud's international outreach branch, said that Obama had *"not been a friend of Israel,"* and that the President's policies had been *"catastrophic."*

Bill Koenig is the publisher of the daily news website watch.org with readers in 105 countries around the world. He is also the author of the book *Eye to Eye: Facing the consequences of dividing Israel.*

CHAPTER TEN

Is It Anti-Arab to be Pro-Israel?

Susan Michael

A growing tendency of some Evangelical leaders in America, particularly Millennial leaders, is to back away from support of Israel for fear that it will be perceived as anti-Arab. And while it is a very good and noble aspiration to not alienate anyone, but rather reach out in love and respect to everyone, this approach demonstrates a lack of understanding of the biblical significance of Israel and of God's plan for the world. Worse yet, it allows cunning anti-Israel activists, who want nothing more than to lead Evangelicals away from support of Israel, to take advantage of these leaders and their movement.

The truth of the matter is that Christians should indeed love and care for all peoples, for truly God loves them, so much so that He sent His only Son to die for them according to John 3:16.

However, it is because of God's love for the world that He brought into existence the nation of Israel through whom He would bring about His plan to redeem that world. His intention was not to bless the Jewish people to the exclusion of the rest of the world, but that through them He would "bless all the families of the earth" (Genesis 12:3). The bequeathing of the land of Canaan as an everlasting possession to Abraham's descendants through Jacob was a critical component of His plan.

To its credit, the American Evangelical Church is trying to come to terms with all of this. And while the pendulum may swing a bit too far one way, solid biblical exegesis, knowledge of historical fact, and accurate analysis can help them find the balance that they aspire to achieve.

The Church's Relationship with the Jewish People

For most of Church history ordinary Christians did not have access to the Bible to even know what it taught. Only those who read Hebrew, Greek or Latin could study it. As a result there were teachings about the Jewish people that simply were not grounded in scripture and produced centuries of anti-Semitism in the heart of Christian Europe. Replacement Theology was the fertile ground for anti-Semitism and the teaching of contempt for the Jewish people that led to their persecution, expulsion, and murder.[1]

However, as soon as the Bible was translated into common languages some 500 years ago, which allowed Christians to read the scriptures for themselves, they discovered the error of their ways attested to by the many promises of God to one day regather the Jewish people back to their ancient homeland. Preachers began to teach about that return, and they prayed for and supported it as an act of justice for a people who had suffered persecution for centuries.

Some of the greatest and most respected Evangelicals in history were what we would call Christian Zionists today: John and Charles Wesley, Charles Haddon Spurgeon, Bishop Ryle of Liverpool, Professor Jacob Janeway of the Scottish National Church and many others.[2] The only difference between them and today's Christian Zionists is that they supported a future event,

---

1 Replacement Theology is the teaching that the Church has replaced the Jewish people in the plans and purposes of God due to their rejection of Jesus' Messianic credentials.

2 For a history of Christian Zionism and quotes from some 50 Christian leaders over the last 500 years who supported the re-establishment of Israel based on their reading of scripture see: www.israelanswers.com/christian_zionism/a_history_of_christian_zionism

while today's Christian Zionists have witnessed the return of the Jews to their homeland and actively support a current event.

While Replacement Theology exists, and is usually the dividing line in the Christian world regarding those who support Israel and those who do not, the Church as a whole has come a very long way in its relations with the Jewish people.

The Church's Relationship with the Arab World

In its relations with the Arab world, however, the Church was not the errant persecutor, but the persecuted. Therefore, the heart change needed to repair this relationship will need to come from Muslim leaders admitting their wrong theology and desire to make amends. In the meantime, the American Evangelical Church has serious problems of its own in its approaches to the Arab world that need to be addressed. First, a word of clarification about terminology is needed.

The term "Arab" is often used broadly, as in this article, but we must recognize that whereas there are roughly 100 million Arabic speaking people in the broader Middle Eastern region, many of them are not ethnically Arab. And whereas the vast majority are Muslims, there has been a significant indigenous Christian population. They are often referred to as "Arab Christians," but most Middle East Christians are not ethnically Arab, only Arabic speaking.

A thousand years ago there were more Christians in the Middle East than in Europe. Even a century ago, more than 20% of the region's population was Christian. Today, estimates put the Christian population of the region at 5% and likely to become extinct if Islamist forces continue to gain power. The second largest Christian community in the Middle East, after the Copts of Egypt, is the Syrian Christians. They are now dispersed, many are homeless refugees, and will never regain their community's size and strength. The Chaldean Christians of Iraq and the surrounding region are facing extinction if ISIS retains control of their lands.

The Evangelical Christian world's concern for these indigenous Middle Eastern Christians has been abysmal. Even today the Church in America is largely silent as millions of Christians in the Middle East face extinction. This is a sin that needs immediate rectification, or surely God will judge this self-centered apathy, and rightly so.

Another fallacy in the Evangelical Church is often a flawed theology toward the Arabic people: they are often discounted as evil and unredeemable. Many a sermon has attempted to blame Ishmael for all the troubles of the Middle East. Because he was a product of Abraham's "mistake," it is implied that He and his descendants are rejected by God and doomed to the violence their society exhibits.

> **Another fallacy in the Evangelical Church is often a flawed theology toward the Arabic people: they are often discounted as evil and unredeemable.**

This sounds vaguely similar to the Church's teachings about the Jews for centuries: cursed by God, rejected, and doomed to the wanderings and persecutions they endured. These types of racial theories are absolutely anathema to the message of John 3:16 that God loves the whole world irrespective of race. No human being is unredeemable.

Rejection of Arabs in general, and ignoring the plight of Arab Christians in particular, is wrong and unbiblical. Equally wrong is allowing the pendulum to swing all the way to the other side and tolerate, if not adopt, the anti-Semitic and anti-Israel ideology of the Muslim world in order to gain their "friendship."

The danger of the "pro-Palestine" movement within Evangelical circles is that the Palestinian Authority is a Muslim-dominated government which is corrupt. It discriminates against Christians, jails and tortures Muslim converts to Christianity, does not allow freedom of speech, and fosters incitement in the public square based on lies about Israel. Is this really what the pro-Palestine Evangelicals are supporting?

To be pro-Israel is to support the existence and security of a fully democratic nation that shares the same Judeo-Christian values as America, such as freedom of speech, freedom of religion, and basic human rights. In fact, it is to support the only government in the Middle East under which the Christian community is growing and thriving. Israel is not perfect, neither is the United States, and Christian supporters are free to criticize aspects of Israeli actions or society. But, to support a Palestinian movement that calls for the destruction of Israel is unacceptable.

Who Really Are God's People in the Middle East?

While there are political, moral, and practical reasons for Christians to support Israel, the biblical foundation known as biblical, or Christian, Zionism, is the belief that God bequeathed the land of Canaan to the Jewish people as an everlasting possession for the purposes of world redemption. [3] The pro-Palestinian sympathizers in the Christian world portray Christian Zionism as heresy, claiming that it politicizes the scriptures.

One of the more vocal Christian theologians leading a campaign against Christian Zionism is Dr. Gary Burge, Professor of New Testament at Wheaton College. His book, "Who are God's people in the Middle East?" laid out a form of Replacement Theology, which claimed that the Church had replaced the Jewish people as the people of God. He concluded that the Palestinian Christians are the real people of God in the Israeli-Arab conflict, arguing that Christians should support them, instead of the Jewish people.

We should indeed love and support our fellow Christians in the Palestinian territories, but this does not require that we discard Israel and invalidate or discredit God's covenant with her. Instead, it requires an honest assessment of the situation facing Palestinian Christians and who is really to blame for it. Burge and others who share his view prefer to simply blame Israel, because it validates their Replacement Theology.

Anyone concerned for the Christians of the Middle East, including Palestinian Christians, should be applauding Israel, the one country in the region where the Christian community is thriving and growing. Israel is the only safe haven in a region where the rights of Christians are secure, as

---

3   For a full treatment of the theology of Christian Zionism see the ICEJ's Biblical Zionism booklet series by Rev. Malcolm Hedding for sale at www.icejusa.org/basis-chrisitian-support-Israel-booklet. Also see "Christian Zionism in Balance " by Rev. Hedding found at www.icejusa.org/christian-zionism-balance or visit www.israelanswers.com

opposed to the Palestinian territories where their numbers are dwindling rapidly.[4] This decline is indicative of the much larger problem of Islamic radicalism facing Christians throughout the Middle East.

Our Christian compassion should not stop with Israel or Middle East Christians. It should include concern for all the peoples of the Middle East. Jesus died for the whole world, including Arab and Muslim peoples, who He loves just as much as anyone else. In fact, the many accounts of Jesus appearing to Muslims today in dreams and visions illustrate just how much God loves them and is revealing Himself to those who have a heart to receive Him.

Being Honest About the Suffering of Palestinians

A true Christian perspective must not only be based on love, and sound biblical exegesis, but also on historical fact. This is challenging because of a prevalent Palestinian narrative that has little regard for historical fact.[5] While the constraints of space in this article do not allow us to discuss all of the political issues associated with the Arab-Israeli conflict, it is important to briefly examine the issues of justice and claims

In 1999, Israel turned over control of the major areas populated by Palestinians to the Palestinian Authority (PA), in accordance with the Oslo Peace Accords, so that 99% of Palestinians are ruled by their own government. Israel does maintain border control and check-points within the West Bank, and we recognize that these security measures produce difficulties for the Palestinian people. However, the real cause for their suffering is not Israel's security measures, but the culture of terrorism and the corruption of the Palestinian leadership who are benefiting from the continuing conflict. As a result, these leaders refuse to sit down at the negotiating table with Israel to secure a better future for their people.

---

4   See Father Gabriel Naddaf's statement to the UN Human Rights Council: http://www.cnsnews.com/news/article/lauretta-brown/priest-un-israel-only-safe-place-christians-middle-east.

5   Palestinian leaders perpetrate such lies as: the Holocaust never happened, the first and second temples never existed in Jerusalem, Al-Aksa Mosque is in danger of collapse due to Israel, and that Jesus was a Palestinian. Such blatant lies are found throughout their speeches as well as school textbooks and government supported media.

The Palestinian people have suffered grave injustices, but primarily at the hands of their own leaders. While there are Palestinians who lost their lives and homes in the 1948 War of Independence, the continuing oppression of the Palestinian people by their own Arab leaders is a travesty.[6]

If Palestinian leaders had partnered with Israel, they would have established an independent state that could be the most prosperous, free, and advanced Arab country in the region. However, under the Palestinian Authority, there is no freedom of speech or freedom of the press, children are taught to hate and murder Jews beginning in kindergarten, the unemployment rate remains exceedingly high, and impoverished Palestinian refugees still live in camps. Year after year, billions of dollars in international aid earmarked for the Palestinian people are siphoned off by corrupt leaders.[7]

This is the injustice inflicted upon the Palestinian people that Israel's detractors will not acknowledge. Ascribing all blame to Israel and ignoring blatant injustices perpetrated by the Arab leaders, is not only dishonest – it is indicative of underlying anti-Semitic sentiment.

God's Love For All The World

God's love for the world is why He brought into existence the nation of Israel through whom He would bring about His great plan to redeem that world. Their role in His plan would afford them a place of preservation and promised blessing. Their calling would also place them directly in the line of fire, and consequently there would be much suffering throughout the centuries because of it. The story of the Jewish people is filled with exiles, persecutions, pogroms, expulsions and attempts at annihilation. There is no explanation for this history other than the biblical role bequeathed to them by God.

---

6   See The Arabs' Historic Mistakes in Their Interactions with Israel by Canadian-Lebanese writer Fred Maroun at http://www.gatestoneinstitute.org/8388/arabs-israel-historic-mistakes

7   For statistics and photographs contrasting the Palestinian elite's opulence with the abject poverty of refugees they refuse to absorb please see: http://jcpa.org/article/luxury-alongside-poverty-in-the-palestinian-authority/. For similar treatment of the Gaza Strip please see: https://www.washingtonpost.com/world/middle_east/gaza-middle-class-discovers-spin-classes-fine-dining-private-beaches/2015/08/23/7e23843c-45d5-11e5-9f53-d1e3ddfd0cda_story.html.

Psalm 83:1-4 explains that, as a consequence, they are in the line of fire in a war against God Himself. "O God… those who hate you…have said 'Come, and let us cut them off from being a nation, that the name of Israel may be remembered no more.'" God knew that the people of Israel would pay a price and their history would be full of suffering. This could explain why He promised blessings on any who would bless and help them.

The story of Israel is not a story about a people more loved or blessed than others, but the story of God's love for the world, and His initiative to use the lineage of Abraham, Isaac and Jacob to redeem and adopt that world into His family. God did not exclude Ishmael or anyone else from His blessings, but He did set them aside while He established the lineage of His people and carried out His plan to "bless all the families of the earth" with redemption.

The story of Israel is not a story about a people more loved or blessed than others, but the story of God's love for the world, and His initiative to use the lineage of Abraham, Isaac and Jacob to redeem and adopt that world into His family.

After Muslim leaders have used the story of Ishmael to instill rejection, jealously, and resentment in billions of Muslims, God Himself is reaching out to their followers letting them know that they have not been rejected and can be part of His family as well. Thousands of Muslims are having dreams and visions of Jesus and accepting Him as Savior. Immediately, their hearts are filled with love. This author knows a number of Muslim background converts and every one of them has a love for the Jewish people, because they recognize they have been adopted into the family as siblings.

Conclusion

The Arab-Israeli conflict is one of the most complex issues today made up of intertwining factors that are theological, historical, and political. They are also personal and often emotional for those directly affected. Therefore, a Christian approach to the Arab-Israeli conflict must be one not only grounded in love for all the people involved, but one that is biblically founded, and discerns between what is historical fact and politically motivated mistruths. One will then understand that the greatest blessing for the Arab people is found in God's covenant with the people of Israel. Therefore, it is absolutely pro-Arab to be pro-Israel.

Susan Michael has spent the past thirty years developing the International Christian Embassy Jerusalem in the United States and around the world. She currently serves as the ministry's USA Director and is a member of the ICEJ's international Board of Directors.

CHAPTER ELEVEN

Praying for Israel: Why and How

Wendy D. Beckett

You may surmise, as you study the chapters of this book, that to understand the whole subject of Israel requires revelation from God. Actually the truth often comes slowly as one might peel the layers off an onion. People arrive at this truth in many different ways and at different times in their lives.

My journey started in Toronto, Canada, as a child of three sitting on a snowbank arguing with my four year old Jewish friend from across the street. We were in the intense days of World War II and she announced that she hated the Germans. In my childish self-righteousness, I told her we must not hate anyone. Finally she looked me in the eye and declared, "You don't know what they are doing to my people!"

So began my understanding enhanced six years later by the tumultuous birth of the state of Israel. "That must be what the prophets meant," my mother reflected during those early days of Israel's modern history.

I grew up with many Jewish friends and always sensed they were special to God. After marriage and in the midst of raising our six children, my mind and heart were absorbed on the home front. Then in the 1970s my husband and I met leading Bible teachers who did not shrink from proclaiming "the whole counsel of God" Acts 20:27 – including the place of Israel in God's purposes.

For example, they taught from Psalm 102:13 – "You will arise and have mercy on Zion; For the time to favor her, Yes, the set time has come." The Lord was doing "a new thing." Isaiah 43:19. He was favoring Israel in a new way. The layers of the onion began to peel off as we saw in the Word the Lord's great love for His Jewish people. That love has never waned – even through the terrible centuries of persecution they have endured at the hands of the Church.

Why Christians should pray for Israel?

The previous chapters of this book leave no doubt that Israel needs much prayer at this moment in history. Both Israelis and their beloved land are between a rock and a hard place. Almost weekly, news updates bring reports of attacks in restaurants, on buses, at bus stops and on highways. Stabbings occur to innocent hikers, shoppers, at the gates of the Old City, – even a 13 year old girl in her bed.

The Father is allowing a few of the many attempted attacks but those who love this nation are so thankful that "He who keeps Israel shall neither slumber nor sleep" Psalm 121:4. The stories of His divine protection are numerous.

Throughout the Western world, Palestinians are targeting the Church with their message that the trouble in the Middle East is Israel's fault and Christians should boycott, divest and sanction Israel (BDS movement). They say Jews have no right to the land. It belongs to them – the Palestinians.

Since the second century AD, most Christians have bought into a false theology that the Church has replaced Israel. This theory states that all the promises in the Old Testament are now only for the Church. The curses are for the Jewish people. As we have seen, history is full of the devastating consequences of this false doctrine and the resulting anti-Semitism.

Israel will survive. The Scriptures make her destiny sure. However the Father is inviting us to stand with Him in this epic battle for her survival. The Word commands us to "Pray for the peace of Jerusalem" Psalm 122:6. In addition, Isaiah 62:6 declares, "I have set watchmen on your walls, O Jerusalem; they shall never hold their peace (stop praying) day or night." The enemy knows his time is short and he is fighting with all his might. The Lord is enlisting us as watchmen! What a privilege to share with Him as He prepares to bring His Kingdom to earth under His rule.

He must wait "until the restoration of all things, which God has spoken by the mouth of all His holy prophets since the world began" Acts 3:21. The rebirth of the state of Israel in 1948, the reunification of Jerusalem under Israeli rule in 1967, and the ensuing years of the growth of this nation are key events in the prophesied restoration.

To summarize "Why?" we pray for Israel:

- God commands us to pray for the peace of Jerusalem
- God Himself watches over Israel day and night
- The battle for her survival is fierce
- Most Christians don't understand God's purposes for her. Instead they are embracing Replacement Theology
- Certain events need to be prayed into fulfillment before the Messiah can come
- The Father's full blessing will come to the Church only when we stand with Him for His ancient people
- As we allow Him to open our eyes and work His Word in us He creates a heart of compassion -- an urge to pray

Praying for Israel is a privilege – not a duty!

So how does one pray for these dear people so beloved by the Father? What is on the Father's heart for us to pray for? What does it look like when those prayers begin to be answered?

Whole books have been written on how to pray for Israel. The Holy Spirit is so creative He leads us to pray in many unique ways. I once met a lady with such a compassionate heart for the Jewish people that she would pray specifically for Holocaust survivors who were at death's door. She did not know their names but trusted the Lord knew who they were and was answering her prayer. She will not know until eternity the answers to her prayers.

I like to think of those praying for Israel as the group of warriors that Nehemiah stationed around the wall of Jerusalem as it was being rebuilt. In spite of the enemy attacks, those warriors with swords in hand were ready to defend the city (Nehemiah 4). If we are sensitive to the Holy Spirit, He will show us how to pray on our particular part of "the wall." Then all the vulnerable areas will be covered.

> **In spite of the enemy attacks, those warriors with swords in hand were ready to defend the city (Nehemiah 4). If we are sensitive to the Holy Spirit, He will show us how to pray on our particular part of "the wall." Then all the vulnerable areas will be covered.**

One of the best ways to stand in prayer for Israel is to use the Scriptures, "the sword of the Spirit," Ephesians 6:17. Once we are alert to the many applicable verses, they will pop up throughout both the Old and New Testaments. The pages of my well-worn Bible are marked with the hundreds of Scriptures to pray and proclaim (speak out loud) for God's Jewish people. We know when we pray the Word we are praying the Father's heart.

Let's consider three possible ways we may effectively pray.

First, we see He commands us "to pray for the peace of Jerusalem" Psalm 122:6. What does that mean when we have seen anything but peace during the decades since 1948?

We are asking for peace or God's Shalom on the people and the place Jesus called, the "City of the great King" Matt.5:35. When many are truly concentrating prayer there – especially during the major Biblical feasts – terrorists are often discovered before they perpetrate their evil deeds. Many more are thwarted than break through to wound and kill. We can see the result of those prayers.

The Hebrew word, "Shalom" means more than just absence of war and turmoil. When Jewish people greet each other with "Shalom," they mean, "May you have total well-being – body, soul and spirit." So we are asking God for a very full-orbed blessing on Jerusalem and her people – and by extension the whole of Israel. Her economic growth through the last six decades is a great answer to that prayer.

We are also seeking the mighty, visible Kingdom of God to come to earth with the King ruling over His city. May "Your Kingdom come" (Luke 11:2) as it will be at the end of this age.

Let's ask the Father for the full "Shalom" to come to Israelis – both in Jerusalem and throughout the Land. May the vision of that coming Kingdom penetrate our spirits and stir our prayers!

A second major way to pray is for the prophesied return of the Jewish people to the land that was promised to them "as an everlasting covenant" Genesis 17:7.

I work with Operation Exodus, one of the Christian organizations that assist the Jewish people to return "home." This immigration back to Israel is called "aliyah." The Hebrew word means "let us go up" and is used in Psalms 120-134, called Psalms of Ascent – for use as the pilgrims made their way up to Jerusalem for the feasts.

Most of the aliyah ministries began in the 1990s after the Communist wall fell. At first we concentrated primarily on those who had been so oppressed in Russia and its satellite states during the years of communism. Gradually the works have grown to offer assistance to Jewish people from many different parts of the world including in the last few years those in the U.S. needing a little help to make such an uprooting move.

Jeremiah repeats in both chapters 16:14,15 and 23:7,8 that an exodus is coming that will overshadow the one out of Egypt, the historic exodus under Moses. Between Israel's rebirth in 1948 and the end of 2015, 3.2 million Jewish immigrants have returned home. However the greatest aliyah is yet to come!

Operation Exodus has compiled more than 40 Scriptures from the Prophets alone which describe the return of the Jewish people to their ancient land in the last days. Over and over the Lord says, "I will gather them back!" We are very aware that we are only His hands, feet and mouthpiece. What a joy to receive frequent letters of gratitude from the new immigrants as they acknowledge God's faithfulness in carrying them through many obstacles to settle them in the cities and towns of Israel!

So let's pray, "Gather the Jewish people home and 'plant them in their own land, never again to be uprooted'" Amos 9:15.

So let's pray, "Gather the Jewish people home and 'plant them in their own land, never again to be uprooted'" Amos 9:15. In Jeremiah 32:37 and 41 we encounter a compelling image of the Father's heart for them. "I will surely gather them from all the lands where I banished them...and will assuredly plant them in this land with all My heart and soul." This Scripture is the only one in the whole Bible describing the Lord working "with all My heart and soul."

The third major need for prayer is that the people of Israel – in fact all Jewish people – would come into their full inheritance also promised throughout the Prophets. Recently I was so encouraged to learn that many in Israel are crying out for a great spiritual awakening. A few indications this is beginning to happen are giving impetus to these prayers. A new openness and spiritual hunger among Israelis surely must be an answer to thousands of prayers through the centuries. What a privilege to join with them to see the Lord bring spiritual restoration to His beloved people!

In the following Scriptures we see the Lord drawing back the curtain to reveal His answer to our prayers:

"They will sparkle in his land like jewels in a crown" Zechariah 9:16 (NIV)

"I will grant salvation to Zion, My splendor to Israel" Isaiah 46:13 (NIV)

"...your eyes will see Jerusalem, a peaceful abode, a tent that will not be moved; ...There the Lord will be our Mighty One" Isaiah 33:20,21 (NIV)

"Sing, O Daughter of Zion; shout aloud, O Israel! Be glad and rejoice with all your heart, O Daughter of Jerusalem! ... The Lord, the King of Israel, is with you; never again will you fear any harm... He is mighty to save" Zephaniah 3:14-16 (NIV)

To summarize three possible ways to pray for Israel:

1. For the peace of Jerusalem – with the Hebrew understanding of "Shalom"

2. For the prophesied return of the Jewish people to their Land to be complete

3. For Jewish people in Israel and throughout the world to come into their full, promised inheritance.

May we cause the Father's heart to rejoice! May the volume and depth of prayer for this people He loves "with an everlasting love" (Jeremiah 31:3) bring to completion "the restoration of all things" (Acts 3:21) and the coming of Messiah!

Wendy Beckett is the US Prayer Coordinator for Operation Exodus-Ebenezer Emergency Fund. She is also the author of the book, *God Keeps Covenant: A Thirty-Day Study on God's Love for Israel.*

AFTERWORD
The Legacy of Ed McAteer

Daniel Johnson & Thomas Lindberg

There was a man sent from God. His pastor described him as a "man among men and one man in a million." Never taken by surprise, the sovereign God has a way of raising up a man or woman in the darkest hour to stand in the gap, to build a wall, to plug the dike against impending doom. It may be the boy Samuel, a prophet like Ezekiel or Daniel, or in our day a Bonhoeffer, Charles Colson, or Billy Graham. Such a man was Edward Eugene McAteer, an orphan boy who rose to dizzying heights in his career only to abandon those heights for a higher calling.

A man is identified by his priorities. Ed McAteer's priorities were never in doubt: God, family, country—and a robust, uncompromising love for the Jewish people and the State of Israel. Good-humored, gracious, endowed with hearty and infectious laughter, he could also be tough. He was intransigent when it came to truth. Equivocation was not an option. It never occurred to him to beat around the bush. Courage was a way of life. You couldn't help but love him, but don't try to move him away from those rock-bottom principles that formed the foundation of his life. He would have agreed with Os Guinness who said, "We respect the right to be wrong. But we also insist that the principle of 'the right to believe anything' does not not lead to the conclusion that 'anything anyone believes is right.'"

Who was this man and what were the building blocks God used to prepare him to mobilize Evangelicals to pay attention to their civic responsibilities at a time when the nation was making bad decisions? What gave rise to his love for Jewish people and his insistence that the "land" was not for sale? And how do you account for the unswerving loyalty to Scripture which left him with no alternative than to obey implicitly every word he read in the Book—and the courage to withstand criticism, to resist the temptation to get along at any cost? "You have enemies?" Winston Churchill asked, "Good! That means you've stood for something, sometime in your life."

Ed McAteer was born in the John Gaston Hospital in Memphis, Tennessee on July 29, 1926. His mother died when he was four. His father traveled the world in the Merchant Marines and was never home. Letters came from time to time but father and son met only twice. The siblings were farmed out to relatives and friends and Ed found a home with his mother's sister and her husband. The loss of a mother and a father can leave a youngster at loose ends, but two things happened for Ed that literally saved his soul and shaped his life. At the age of fifteen he accepted the invitation of a friend to visit the local Methodist church. When the pastor summoned sinners to the altar, Ed responded, surrendered his life to Christ, embraced the gospel and began a relationship with a heavenly Father, a relationship that would have profound implications for his life and for countless lives he would touch.

The second thing that happened by the grace of God was a girl called Faye. Ed McAteer fell in love with Faye Carter from Crocket County. She became a lifelong partner and companion and mother of their two sons. Ed would have told you that he could not have accomplished what God enabled him to do were it not for the love, encouragement and prayers of Faye Carter McAteer.

His biographer traced the steps of Ed McAteer from the boxing ring to the sea, from classroom to career with a billion-dollar company. His unbounded energy found relief in the game of boxing, but it was no relief for his opponents. He loved the sport and excelled in it. Service in the United States

Navy was both thrilling and hazardous. He never forgot the Battle of Leyte in 1944 when their floating home and beloved ship the St. Lo was struck by a Kamikaze pilot and sank in twenty-eight minutes. Later, Ed commended, "I'm proud to say I served my country when she needed me, like millions of others. I love the United States of America." For his courageous service Ed was awarded the Presidential bronze star by the Navy Department.

Following discharge from the Navy, Ed enrolled in law school. Job search led him to an employment agency that was a turning point in his life. The interviewer saw in the young man something they liked and offered him a job in sales. "That's a long way from law," Ed said. "You're right," replied the interviewer, "but we see in you the right personality to be good at sales." For the next twenty years Ed would be the top salesman with the Colgate Company and one day hold the job of the man who first interviewed him.

Those were good years for the orphan boy who grew up without mother or father: promotions, salary increases, benefits, two new cars in the garage, a lovely family, satisfying activity in his church—the best of times. But there was a growing unease about his beloved country. Two hundred years of history slipping away. The secularization of the culture. Spending by local and federal government out of control. The Bible and prayer removed from school, and deeply disturbing to the former toothpaste salesman was the legalization of abortion. Ed remembered the words of G. K. Chesterton who long ago warned, "We're always near the breaking point when we care only for what is legal and nothing for what is lawful." Passing laws until you're blue in the face does not make wrong right. And Ed was troubled.

Ed was troubled because he was a student of American history. Almost to his dying day he and Faye would regularly read some chapters out of our history along with their Bible reading. For example, he recalled the words of George Washington, who in his first inaugural address in 1789 said, "The propitious smiles of heaven cannot be expected on a nation that disregards the eternal rules of order and the right which heaven itself has ordained."

You don't build a tree; you plant a tree. It grows. Growth requires good soil, rain, sunshine, oxygen—and time. And time is required for a civilization to rise and flourish. But as freedom is never more than one generation away from extinction, so a civilization, a culture can be dismantled in one generation. Uncouple the weakest link and the strongest chain is broken. The blood, sweat, and tears of the centuries can be undone in one careless generation. Dismayed by the work of the wrecking crew, but never in despair, Ed set out to do something. He gathered round him some of the top leaders in the country in business, politics, and religion and formed what he called the Religious Roundtable, an organization dedicated to American renewal.

But more and more in Ed's mind appeared a linkage between a strong United States of America and a stable and secure State of Israel. As a youth, Ed was introduced to a unique promise. In a conversation with Faye's grandfather, Genesis 12 grabbed his attention. God made a promise to bless Abraham and bless those who blessed him. And there was something about the "land" that seemed important. God gave to Abraham and to his family the land of Israel. That promise was repeated over and over throughout the Old Testament and never rescinded; Ed McAteer was not only trained in law but was a firm believer in the Word of God. A homeland for the Jews made good sense on a number of levels but first and foremost was the promise God had made to Abraham long ago and recorded in the Book Ed came to love. That settled it, case closed.

Something about the Jewish people and the State of Israel provokes an irrational hatred, inflaming passions, inciting riots, fueling wars and rumors of wars—and enough of the lie of moral equivalence suggesting that Israel be cautious in response to terrorist rockets, demanding the Jewish nation be restrained in dealing with determined terrorists. Still, the centuries of dislocation, deprivation, imprisonment, the threat of assimilation—and the wandering years, which saw their character maligned, their synagogues burned, their cemeteries defaced have not altered but rather underscored the fact that they are here to stay. Like the bush that burned but was not consumed, the Jew endures—and Ed McAteer would be their friend. That friendship would cost him dearly. Friends and supporters who didn't agree with his attempt to rouse a sleeping church and rally Evangelicals to pray for, stand with, and support the State of Israel would desert and withdraw funds from the Roundtable, but Ed would not be deterred. He had no choice.

Ever the historian, Ed recalls the fiasco in the 1930s which culminated in the Second World War. The British Prime Minister Neville Chamberlain meets with Adolf Hitler in Munich seeking to tone things down, to come to some kind of agreement about claims and counter-claims in Eastern Europe. Chamberlain returns to England with the promise of "peace in our time." He is accorded a hero's welcome. He is invited to Buckingham Palace and then in Parliament he addresses the people, "My friends, I believe it is peace in our time. Now I recommend you go home and sleep quietly in your beds."

Winston Churchill had warned the world about what he saw, but few listened. On one occasion, addressing Parliament, he said, "Laugh, but listen." They laughed but did not listen. But no one was laughing when two years later the German Luftwaffe began a months-long bombing of London.

Like Churchill, Ed could read the writing on the wall. The Jewish people were once more under assault, their homeland threatened, and it was time to rally Christians in America to remember Abraham. And remember God's promise. To Ed McAteer, this is no time to "go home and sleep quietly in your beds."

Charles Kettering said of the Wright brothers that they "flew through the smokescreen of impossibility." So did Ed McAteer, the orphan boy, some of whose last words we remember, "The reason I stay in the battle is because anything is possible with God. It makes no difference whether He saves by few or by many…it's always too soon to quit."

Daniel Johnson is the author of numerous books, including *Come Home America*. Thomas Lindberg is the Pastor of First Assembly Memphis. Together, they co-authored *The Power of One, The Ed McAteer Story*.